The Illustrated Guide to

DREAMS

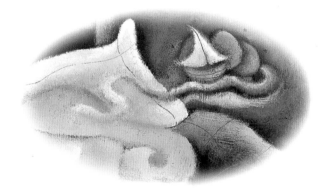

The Illustrated Guide to

DREAMS

BRENDA MALLON

 A GODSFIELD BOOK

Library of Congress Cataloging-in-Publication Data Available

10 9 8 7 6 5 4 3 2 1

Published in 2000 by Sterling Publishing Company, Inc.
387 Park Avenue South, New York, N.Y. 10016
© 2000 Godsfield Press
Text © 2000 Brenda Mallon

Designed for Godsfield Press by
The Bridgewater Book Company

Studio Photography: Ian Parsons
Illustrations: Arlene Adams, Michaela Bloomfield,
Liz Cooke, Nicola Evans
Picture Research: Liz Eddison

Distributed in Canada by Sterling Publishing
c/o Canadian Manda Group, One Atlantic Avenue, Suite 105
Toronto, Ontario, Canada M6K 3E7
Distributed in Australia by Capricorn Link (Australia) Pty Ltd
P O. Box 6651, Baulkham Hills, Business Centre, NSW 2153, Australia

Printed and bound in China

Sterling ISBN 0–8069–2773–9

Contents

Introduction

Each night we spend two and a half hours in a very special world of dreamscapes filled with amazing images. In that world of dreams, treasures are unearthed, uncharted places are explored, and new truths are revealed.

But dreams are more than just amazing experiences; they are essential to our mental health. We cannot live without dreaming. In experiments where people have been prevented from dreaming, they quickly become emotionally unbalanced, their ability to think clearly is damaged, and they exhibit signs of great distress. Dreams help us to process all the information we receive when awake. They help us to solve problems, appreciate the dynamics of relationships, develop self-awareness, enhance creativity, and connect to the universal dimension of existence. Dreams warn us, guide us, help us to recover from a broken heart and discover new strengths.

What do your dreams mean? Which are the truly significant dreams? Are they only those that come at a particular point in the nightly dream cycle, which follows the rhythms from lighter to deeper rapid-eye-movement (REM) sleep? Or are they also those visions that come to us during moments of pure peace—moments when we look

Dreams provide us with the opportunity to live our wildest fantasies, such as traveling the world or experiencing great wealth.

Nightmares allow us to discharge negative energy and relieve tension.

HOW TO USE THIS BOOK

The purpose of this book is to help you gain entry to the mysterious world of dreams. The dream world is a vast domain. It has been part of human development since the earliest times in all cultures and in all spiritual practices. Chapter 1, "Historical overview," presents a short historical summary of the role dreams have played in various cultures throughout history, and provides an insight into present-day research and theories on the subject of dreaming.

Keeping a journal beside your bed will help you record your dreams. It will help you recognize dream patterns.

Before you can begin to interpret your dreams, you must first remember them. Chapter 2, "Recording your dreams," offers techniques that will help you remember your dreams and advice on how to keep a dream journal. Your journal will make it possible to recognize the recurrence of significant images and patterns in your dream life.

Although each person's dream is a unique experience, there are certain dream symbols that we all share. This universality of the dream state is explored in Chapter 3, "The language of symbols." If you cannot find the specific theme of your dream in this list of dream symbols and themes, then look under the most closely related topic. For instance, if you dream of a cottage, for which there is no entry, look at the "house" entry to help you understand the symbolic significance of your dream.

inward and tune into another dimension? Whatever the answer, it is your own personal perception of your dreams that is the crucial factor in their interpretation. No two dreams are ever exactly the same, even though they may be very similar. Your dream is unique to you; it is a personal communication from yourself to yourself.

All of your dreams are theatrical productions in which you, the dreamer, are script writer, scene setter, actor, prompt, producer, director, and audience. You choose the location, the lighting, the colors, and the mood. You even produce your nightmares, perhaps to force yourself to acknowledge the importance of a particular experience or, as is often the case with theater, to help you discharge negative energy and relieve tension. When interpreting these theatrical productions from the dream world, try not to impose a logical, linear explanation. Be open to the unexpected and the irrational; trust your intuitive responses. Learn from the patterns of your dreams and use the language of metaphors, puns, and allegories to expand your awareness.

Dreams can foretell events, reveal the unknown and enable us to relive the past.

You alone can unlock the full meaning of your dreams. Honest self-appraisal is the first step.

Learning to interpret your own dreams is challenging. It involves a good deal of detective work and honest self-appraisal. However, it is important to remember that you alone hold the key to unlocking the meanings of your dreams. Your dreams are yours. You are the only one who has intimate knowledge of your dreams, so you are the best person to understand their true meaning in your life.

Dreams enable us to see into the future, the past, and the unknown. Chapter 4, "Psychic dreams," shows how dreams can take us into a realm that transcends our normal waking consciousness.

Dreams can be a source of inspiration. In the dream world we may be presented with solutions to problems that plague our progress at work or our creative life; they offer positive strategies to enhance our waking life. This aspect of the dream world is explored in Chapter 5, "Dreams and creativity."

Some diagnostic dreams indicate illness before there are any obvious physical symptoms and give guidance for recovery. Many people have experienced healing dreams in which they have been treated by a "dream doctor" or touched by a beneficent spirit. Chapter 6, "Dreams and health," discusses the connections between dreams and our physical and mental well-being. The final chapter, "Enriching your dream life," gives practical advice and helpful tips on how you can enhance your dream life and, therefore, your waking life.

Throughout the book there are first-hand accounts of other people's dreams and the meaning and significance they held for the dreamer. These examples illustrate how essential dreams are in helping us come to a deep understanding of ourselves and our life situation. You may also find a common experience.

Whether you are a complete beginner in dream interpretation or someone who has been working on dreams for some time, *The Illustrated Guide to Dreams* will enable you to gain entry to this mysterious, inspiring world of dreams and will be a wonderful companion on your voyage of discovery and enhanced self-awareness.

All day we receive packages of information through our senses or thoughts. We cannot sort them all during the day, consciously, so at night our dreams are the mechanism in the packaging room that sorts out what these packages are and where they go in the subconscious. Those bits of information that are most important to us are marked urgent—those are the dreams we remember!

Chris

My dreams are helpful because they let me experiment with things I wouldn't have the courage to do in normal daily life. They are useful for exploring my fantasies.

David

Basically, dreaming is a road to freedom, you can do what you want when you want while dreaming. It's free time for you to use as you desire...I can take chances I wouldn't normally take in day-to-day situations, and make decisions I couldn't make in everyday life.

Kim

Sometimes I may be worrying subconsciously and dreams help me to sort out these worries and do something constructive about solving the problem. For instance, when I overload myself with work and convince myself that I can cope, my dreams tell me how I really feel. So I listen to them and do not overwork so often. They are also an outlet for anger and frustration but they are important to me because I enjoy dreaming.

Emma

Dreams give me ideas and make me think of things I might otherwise omit. They keep me in touch with how I feel. They warn me of illness. They warn me when my periods are coming, which is useful since my cycle is irregular.

Saskia

1 | HISTORICAL OVERVIEW

Humankind has been fascinated by the world of dreams for centuries—since ancient times the imagery and symbolism of dreams have been recorded and analyzed. The first book of dreams, The Oneirocritica, *dating from the second century* CE, *remains a classic of dream interpretation to this day. The ancient Greeks believed that important messages from the gods were contained within dreams and used them to predict the future or even diagnose illness and find cures.*

Although dreams feature significantly in the Bible, the Church later rejected dream interpretation as the work of the devil. Today we are just as intrigued by our dreams as our ancestors were.

1: Historical overview

THE ONEIROCRITICA

The Oneirocritica or *The Interpretation of Dreams*—one of the first dream books ever written and the second book to be printed on the Gutenberg press in the mid-15th century—was compiled by Artemidorus, who was born in Asia Minor in the 2nd century CE. He recorded all the dream wisdom from Babylonian, Assyrian, and Egyptian folklore, for at that time, seeking guidance from dreams was an everyday practice. *The Oneirocritica* was the first comprehensive book, five volumes in all, on the interpretation of dreams and was the most important book on dreams right up to the 19th century.

Artemidorus's ideas on dreams were very close to modern views. He believed that dreams were unique to the dreamer and were affected by the person's occupation, social standing, and health: "If we wish to interpret a dream correctly, we need to take a note of whether the person dreaming it is male or female, healthy or sick, a free man or slave, rich or poor, young or old."

Artemidorus, born in Asia Minor, 2nd century CE. He compiled one of the first books about dream interpretation, The Oneirocritica.

THE ANCIENT GREEKS

Throughout antiquity there was a belief that dreams had a divine origin and carried messages from the gods. The ancient Greeks believed that the great god Zeus, god of gods, sent warnings, messages, and prophecies in dreams with the help of Hypnos, the god of sleep, and Morpheus, the god of dreams.

Many Greek philosophers addressed the subject of dreams. Plato (428–347 BCE) recognized that

The ancient Greeks believed that dreams contained messages, warnings and prophecies from the various gods.

dreams could radically influence waking actions and gave as an example the fact that Socrates studied music and the arts because a dream had instructed him to do so. Aristotle (384–322 BCE) attempted to study dreams in a rational way. He argued that so-called prophetic dreams were simply coincidences and put forward the argument that the most skillful interpreter of dreams is "he who has the faculty for absorbing resemblances," that is, the person who could make connections between waking events, the society at large, and the life history of the dreamer. Aristotle also believed that dreams could reflect the physical state of the dreamer and could therefore be used as an aid to diagnosis, an idea supported by Hippocrates (c.460–370 BCE).

The ancient Greeks also believed that dreams could influence waking actions. Socrates was inspired to study music as a direct result of a dream.

INCUBATION RITES

A widespread practice among ancient Greeks and Romans was dream incubation. The word "incubation" comes from the Latin word *incubatio*, which means "sleeping in." The aim of dream incubation was to try to stimulate a dream from an oracular or a healing god, such as Asclepius, the Greek god of medicine. A person who wanted an answer to a question or who wanted to be healed physically or emotionally would go to one of the many dream temples. There he or she would take part in ritualistic preparations, incantations, and purification, then spend the night in the sanctuary to incubate a dream. You can learn how to incubate your own dreams later in this book.

Carvings and paintings illustrate the ancient Greeks' interest in dream incubation and the rituals used.

DREAMS AND RELIGION

The Bible contains more than twenty accounts of dreams that refer to divine guidance; some of these dreams changed the course of history. In one of his own dreams, Moses was told of their powerful significance: "Hear now my words," he dreamed. "If there be a prophet among you, I, the Lord, will make myself known to him in a vision and will speak to him in a dream." (Num.12:6)

Early Christian writers believed that God revealed himself through dreams.

The first Christians accepted the idea that dreams could come from a supernatural source, but for them the source was not the gods of the ancient Greeks, but the one true Christian God. Early Christian writers such as Tertullian (155–222 CE) recognized the value of dreams, saying that God "especially intended dreams to be of particular assistance in natural foresight."

St. John Chrysostom (347–407 CE) preached that God revealed himself through dreams. Also, unusual for a man of his time, he stated that we are not responsible for our dreams, so we should not be ashamed of the images and actions they contain, particularly explicitly sexual dreams.

St. Augustine (354–430 CE) was one of the first to realize that part of the psyche (the human mind or soul) must remain unconscious, hidden from the person except in dreams. "I cannot grasp all that I am," he said. He was afraid God would hold him responsible for his dreams, and these, especially the lustful ones, were beyond his control. The mother of St. Augustine "saw" his conversion in one of her dreams, nine years before it happened.

Over time, the Church's attitude toward dreams became less

tolerant. By the 13th century, dreams, especially sexual dreams, were seen as the work of the devil. The Church was the interpreter of God's word, so any revelation given to an individual in a dream was seen as satanic. Martin Luther (1483–1546 CE), the founding father of Protestantism, endorsed this view. In his eyes sin was "the confederate and father of foul dreams."

Many prominent Christians in the Middle Ages held a different view and thought that dreams were the work of the devil.

DANIEL'S INTERPRETATION

Nebuchadnezzar, king of Babylon from 60 BCE, dreamed that he saw a tall, strong tree standing at the center of the earth; at the base was exquisite foliage, which sheltered wild beasts. Then a messenger from heaven ordered the great tree to be cut down and the king chained to its stump to live like a beast.

Daniel was summoned to interpret the king's dream. He explained that the tree represented the power and glory of the king, but his abasement, to live among the beasts, was sent to teach him that God was as high above Nebuchadnezzar as the king was above the beasts that sheltered beneath him.

In King Nebuchadnezzar's dream, having to live as a beast among beasts could also have served to remind him of humility.

2 | RECORDING YOUR DREAMS

With their vivid imagery, dreams can seem very real at the time but are so easily forgotten upon waking. This chapter shows you how—with a notebook, pen, and a little self-discipline—you can record your dreams in detail. Once you get into the habit of keeping a dream journal you will be enthralled by how even the most seemingly insignificant detail can point to a hidden message for your waking life.

The techniques used here will help you to analyze the details in your dreams from a different perspective and understand the significance of their complex symbolism. Persevere and your dream journal will make fascinating reading for many years to come.

☽ | 2: Recording your dreams

*The seeker after truth eventually has
to investigate himself.*

KIERKEGAARD (1813–55)

KEEPING A DREAM JOURNAL

Keeping a dream journal is the best technique for gaining an understanding of the gift of self-knowledge your dreams provide. But in order to record your dreams, you must first remember them. If you have difficulty remembering your dreams, use the affirmations given on page 118 to set up the most helpful conditions to influence dream recall. Some people vividly remember six or seven dreams a night; others recall one a week. However, the very intention of recording your dreams influences both their frequency and intensity. Many people find that keeping a dream journal trains them to remember more dreams.

Getting started

For your dream journal indulge yourself with a notebook or a sketchbook with a gorgeous cover and paper that is beautiful to the touch. This confirms that you believe your dreams are valuable and worthy of attention. Plain paper will give you more opportunity to include illustrations—you'll be surprised at some of the images that arise. Often, the act of sketching an image will enable you to make a more precise interpretation of your dreams.

Next you need a free-flowing pen and a flashlight to use if you wake from a dream in the middle of the night and do not wish to disturb your sleeping companion by turning on a lamp.

Before you go to sleep

Write the date at the top of the left-hand sheet of a double page (the right-hand side will be used for interpretation). Next to it write your location. Location can affect dreams; for instance, if you are sleeping at your lover's home you may find that your dreams are different from those dreamed in the bedroom where you slept as a child.

When you wake

As soon as you wake, record your dream on the left-hand page of the journal. If you cannot remember the dream in its entirety, record the fragments you do remember, or make a note of your mood if you have no memory of the dream at all. Some dreams are like gossamer and slip away, so make a note as soon after the dream as possible. Use key words if you don't have time to record it in full.

Dream title

Now, give your dream a title. It could be a single word or a brief description. Whether it seems inspired or mundane, if the title reflects the basic content of the dream it will help you remember it later. Giving titles to your dreams helps to lodge them in your memory, and you will appreciate new dreams better in light of your old ones.

*Treat yourself to a
beautiful notebook
or sketchbook to
record your dreams.*

Record your dreams as fully as possible to make it easier to identify patterns and problem-solving clues.

Dream order

If you have a very rich dream, or a series of dreams in the night, record the sequence of the dreams. The first and last dreams can contain the most important information and it can prove fruitful to concentrate on these. The final dream, just prior to waking, often provides practical, problem-solving clues relating to earlier dreams. Look for patterns in sequential dreams.

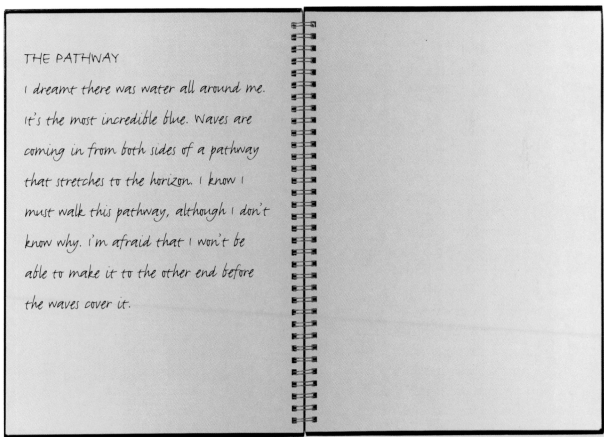

THE PATHWAY

I dreamt there was water all around me. It's the most incredible blue. Waves are coming in from both sides of a pathway that stretches to the horizon. I know I must walk this pathway, although I don't know why. I'm afraid that I won't be able to make it to the other end before the waves cover it.

ACTIVE JOURNAL
WORK TECHNIQUES

Once you have recorded your dreams you are ready to explore their many-layered meanings. The insights gained from dream journals can literally change your life in dramatic ways. The following techniques are designed to help you discover the messages of your dreams. Some techniques will be more fruitful than others, so experiment with all of them and discover which suits you best. They may also inspire you to find your own approach.

Find a quiet space to read your journal. Clear any clutter from a work surface to avoid distractions.

DREAM CHECKLIST

After you have recorded your dream in the journal, ask yourself the following questions and note the answers on the page opposite your dream narrative:

• What was the emotional "feel" of the dream?
  Tense, fearful, happy, neutral?
• What was the atmosphere in the dream?
  Gloomy, bright, foggy, misty?
• What was significant about the colors?
  Vivid, monochrome, pale, and insipid?
• What surprised you most about the dream?
  Its vividness? The feelings it evoked?
• Can you recognize a trigger for the dream?
  A television program, an argument?
• What is your immediate interpretation?
  Your gut feelings about what the dream means.

A wide-eyed and innocent approach

Approach every dream with wide-eyed innocence so that your preconceptions don't get in the way of a meaningful interpretation. Try to eliminate preconceived ideas and be open to the unexpected so that you let the freshness of each dream reach you uncontaminated by assumptions.

The Martian technique

Look at your dream in the simplest way possible, using simple language. Imagine that you are explaining the various elements of your dream to a Martian who has never come across such things before.

Dreaming about competitive sports often symbolizes a competitive nature or situation.

When one of my clients, I'll call him Tony, dreamed of a racing car, I asked, Martian style, "What is a car?" He replied, "It's a means of transportation, to take people from one place to another. It has wheels and an engine, but this one is special, it can go much faster than most cars. It has more power and can be dangerous, especially if it gets into a race with another car." Tony recognized that he was describing his own competitive streak, which was leading him into destructive conflict with a colleague.

The cast

View each member of the dream cast as a part of yourself. If there is a child, for example, ask yourself which childlike part of your personality this represents. Is it the joyous freedom from responsibilities that you would like to feel, or is it the spontaneous child who can have tantrums if he or she wants to? Even if the dream character is someone you know in waking life, consider how it may represent a facet of yourself. For example,

your dream boss, rather than being your real boss from your working life, may symbolize the "bossy" side of your personality.

Dialogue with the dream characters

Imagine that characters or objects from your dream are sitting opposite you in a chair and you can ask them questions. "Why were you trying to frighten me in my dream?" "What can I do to stop you racing out of control?" "Why won't your brakes work?" Let the answers flow; don't try to make them logical. You will be surprised at the inner wisdom that surfaces when you use this technique.

Dream patterns

Look for recurring themes, people, and patterns in your dreams. If you do not understand the significance of a dream message the first time that you experience it, your brain will repeat it in various forms until you do. Try to look for the connections between dreams. You may discover a series of dreams in which a theme is developed over weeks or even years. The theme may have appeared insignificant at first. The next chapter looks at some of these themes and uncovers their symbolic significance.

Anaïs Nin, writer, painter, and companion of Henry Miller and Salvador Dali, kept a lifelong journal in which dreams became the key to her creativity. She used dreams as the inspiration for a number of books, and her extensive dream records and interpretations are worth investigating if you want to see how themes are repeated.

3 | THE LANGUAGE OF SYMBOLS

Now you have learned how to record your dreams, it is time to move on to the language of symbols. There is an immense range of symbols, and this chapter includes some of the more commonly occurring ones. As any dream interpreter will tell you, although each symbol has a particular meaning, its appearance in a dream is significant and personal to the individual dreamer.

This chapter also demonstrates that all is never as it seems in dreams: the subconscious mind works in a different way from the waking mind, so seeing one particular symbol can have many different interpretations. Use this knowledge to discover the lessons your dreams contain for your waking life.

3: The language of symbols

Moons are associated with sleep and darkness. A full moon can represent the culmination of a project.

Any circular forms that appear in your dreams represent continuity. Wheels can also indicate journeys, or they can symbolize cycles and their completion.

Wedding rings also signify continuity, yet they also represent eternity and wholeness, as well as the firm establishment of a relationship.

Each dreamer is a unique individual with a unique history. Consequently, every dream image has, first and foremost, a personal resonance for the individual. As we explore dreams further, we discover other facets that add to their complexity. At one level, dreams reflect our social conditions —where we live, the food we eat, the language we speak, and so on. At another level, known as the "collective unconscious," dreams depict symbols that have a common meaning based on the shared experiences of humanity. These symbols appear throughout history, in various cultures and myths around the world.

Dreams are full of symbols, each one combining a whole range of ideas, emotions, and knowledge. The symbolic language is unlimited. It uses an infinite variety of puns, metaphors, symbols, signs, numbers, colors, and shapes. When you understand the language of symbols, you can gain a deeper knowledge of your dream world and your waking life.

What follows is a list of some of the most commonly occurring dream symbols and dream themes. Many of the symbols discussed here are ones that I have met again and again in my dream research and dream therapy. But it is important to remember that, although these symbols have a universally recognized meaning, they need to make sense in your world if they are to have significance for you. Consider them, use them as clues, and let them enhance your personal development and creativity. Using this universal language of symbols, you can examine your dreams and build up a personal dream directory that is uniquely yours.

ARCHETYPES

Swiss psychiatrist Carl Jung (1875–1961) introduced the term "archetype" to describe inherited images that come spontaneously from the deepest parts of our unconscious mind and the transcendent level of the soul. Archetypes are constantly recurring symbols found across all cultures, classes, races, and religions. These pictorial images are part of the collective unconscious common to all human beings, and appear in literature, myths, fairy stories, and art from earliest times to the present day.

Archetypes often appear in "big dreams," the emotionally-charged or awe-inspiring ones that are impossible to forget, which often come at a point of change in the dreamer's life. Their intense clarity seems to carry wisdom from outside, from a higher source, from something or someone beyond the dreamer. Such a dream feels enormously significant —and it is. Archetypal dreams are linked to core issues such as death and rebirth, the hero's journey, rites of passage, and creation. Some examples of these eternal motifs are the persona, the shadow, the wise woman or wise man, the animus/anima, and the mandala (see page 26).

The persona

The persona is a mask that covers the essential nature of the dreamer. We all wear masks to a certain extent, perhaps to protect privacy or to fit in with the demands of society or work. This in itself is not a problem; however, it becomes a handicap when the mask replaces the self to such an extent that we no longer know who we really are beneath all the roles we take on. For example,

A key archetypal theme is meeting a wise, all-knowing person. This figure could indicate a new direction in life, or impart significant information.

we may delude ourselves into thinking that we are nothing more than the roles we play—the strong, all-providing partner; the saintly parent; the submissive spouse; and so on. In your dreams these roles or masks are sometimes cast aside, leaving you feeling exposed, naked, or rejected in some way.

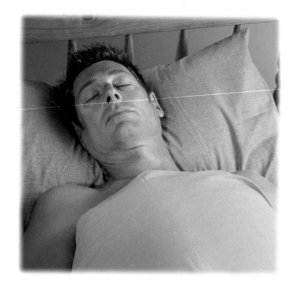

The shadow

This potent archetype represents what we would prefer to deny about our own characters or keep hidden from others. The shadow often appears in dreams as a threatening, mysterious figure, which may be faceless because the dreamer has not yet recognized that aspect of his or her inner self. Dreams show us our shadow side, and situations connected with it, so that we can acknowledge it and set about changing it, or come to terms with it.

Wise woman or wise man

When you meet a wise person in your dreams, it is usually to impart a particular piece of knowledge or to give you directions on how you could go forward in your life. Some dreamers do not see the wise man or woman but hear the wise words as if spoken by a disembodied figure.

Anima/animus

The anima/animus represents the inner qualities that are balancing aspects of gender, so for a woman the animus is her male aspect, and for a male dreamer the anima is his female aspect. The whole self is formed when we can integrate these complementary sides. The anima/animus is to the inner world as the persona is to the outer.

The mandala

A mandala is a symbolic diagram, usually circular or oval, which represents the map of the cosmos in Eastern traditions. Mandalas also symbolize the cycle of life and its unending renewal. These can appear in dreams as flowers, parts of landscape, gardens, or in an object. Any circular forms in your dreams, for example the sun, a stadium, a ring, or a wheel, may represent the mandala. Carl Jung believed that when a mandala appeared in a dream it heralded wholeness and self-integration. It is completion, where the beginning or end are no longer apparent, instead there is a continuous, never-ending eternity.

A mandala is a circular diagram often found in eastern cultures. Any circular forms that appear in your dreams may represent the mandala.

ANIMALS

Animals in dreams frequently represent our basic drives and instincts. They can reflect the wild side of human nature or that which has been domesticated. They sometimes represent the shadow, that part of our nature that has not been subdued and poses some kind of threat.

According to traditional shamanic wisdom, when an animal is dreamed of on three occasions, it signifies that it is a power animal. The shaman can have any number of power animals, or totems as they are also known, but usually he or she would have one particularly significant one.

To the Native Americans, animals were power guides or guardian spirits. To the Aborigines in Australia, they were assistant totems. Each medicine man or woman would appeal to animal guides to assist in their rituals because every animal represented a particular strength or quality. An animal in a dream may bring qualities that the dreamer needs at that time. Is your dream animal your power totem?

To determine the significance of your dream animal ask yourself some questions: Is the animal aggressive or gentle? Submissive or threatening? What qualities can you draw from it?

The following is a list of some of the animals that commonly appear in dreams, carrying with them important symbols and messages:

Bull

The bull, a strong, virile animal, symbolizes masculinity. It also symbolizes power. If you dream of a bull, are you being bullish, unthinkingly rushing into something like a "bull in a china shop" instead of giving yourself time to reflect? Or could the bull refer to a rampant trading market that has a sexual frisson to it? Perhaps the bull stands for a bison, which almost became extinct. Could it represent something in you that feels as if it is being hunted to death?

Cat

Cats are the most independent and sensuous of domesticated pets. However, they can also be "catty," self-centered, and given to attacks on other creatures, sometimes merely for play rather than for survival.

A bull symbolizes the basic instincts of masculinity and drive. Do you feel "bullish" or under threat?

Native Americans believe animals represent particular strengths and qualities.

Dogs

Known as "man's best friend," dogs are noted for their devotion. As guardians they offer protection and service to humans. Dogs can hear and smell things that we cannot, which is why they are used to sniff out drugs and find missing people.

Different breeds have particular characteristics, so if a dog appears in your dream, think about its special abilities or role as it relates to your life at this time. For example, a sheepdog, used for rounding up and guarding sheep, can sometimes "worry" the sheep, and turn against them. Is there someone you are "worrying?"

Elephants

Strength, long memory, faithfulness, and wisdom are all associated with elephants.

Foxes

Fiercely protective, foxes are cunning and resourceful. "Foxed" also means puzzled, so could this mean you are looking for a solution to a problem?

Horses

If you dream of horses, it may be that these animals represent the horses that you ride when awake; but what if you have nothing to do with horses in your waking life? What are they doing in your dreams? The image of a horse that is tamed and controlled but not broken can symbolize our ability to manage our instinctual drives and primitive passions.

The ancient Greek Artemidorus said that horses were particularly common in women's

JANE'S DREAM

*I am asked to ride a huge carthorse
that is plunging and thrashing.
I refuse but feed it, feeling very scared.
It goes free but dies because of my
feeding. It makes terrible death noises.*

dreams. Jane had a dream in which the conflict between the tamed and more instinctual side takes on life and death proportions (see below left).

A carthorse is normally quiet and totally reliable though highly powerful, but in Jane's dream it behaves like an unbroken stallion. There is a further contradiction with the feeding: the act of nourishment causes death not growth.

Some psychologists say horses represent male sexuality—the stud—while riding a horse is commonly linked to the act of sexual intercourse. This is another element Jane could investigate as she works on her dream.

Rats

These creatures, who are shy of the light and who live in the underworld, are often associated with underhand dealings. Also, to "rat" on someone is to give information that will cause problems. Does this fit in with any of your relationships?

Snakes

Snakes in many ancient cultures were associated with seduction and femininity, and with Persephone, Hecate, and the awesome Medusa, who had live snakes on her head in place of hair.

The serpent in the Biblical creation story is also firmly embedded in our minds, with its connotation of corruption and seduction. However, it is also associated with the spiritual energy that is believed to lie dormant at the base of the human spine, known as "the base chakra" or by the Sanskrit word *kundalini*, which means "serpent fire."

A snake's ability to shed its skin has come to symbolize renewal and regeneration and consequently is associated with healing. The medical symbol of two snakes intertwining on the staff of Mercury highlights the creature's contrasting power. Medicine, like snakes, can bring both life and death, renewal or destruction.

ANIMAL PUNS

Language is so rich and multilayered that it can offer more than one interpretation; for example, an ass can be an animal used for transport, a fool, or a person's backside. A bear is a symbol of healing and strength. However, a dream bear may represent other meanings, including "bare." Are you feeling exposed or vulnerable? Baring your soul? What burden are you having to bear? Is there something you are faced with that makes you feel unable to cope?

Dreams can prepare the dreamer for the changes in lifestyle and responsibility that a new baby brings, and can also help the dreamer to cope with the nurturing role of being a parent.

BABIES

Babies in dreams may indicate an interest in pregnancy, newborn children, or fertility. When a baby appears in your dreams it may be because you are pregnant, or want to be, or because you have a young child. A dream baby may also represent a new beginning or fresh start in your life, such as moving home, changing job, or embarking on a new relationship. It may also indicate a new, creative development in your life —your "brain child."

The appearance of babies in dreams often coincides with the development of a dormant side of your character or a new skill. It is quite common for both men and women to dream about babies.

Dreaming during pregnancy

There are many anxieties that surface during pregnancy and after the birth, as discussed in the section on pregnancy (see pages 60–61), but such dreams are quite normal during this period of change. Natalie's dream is not unusual:

I had a recurring dream in pregnancy that I had had a baby but forgot about it for several days so that, when I went back to it, it had died of neglect and starvation.

This series of dreams emphasized the important nurturing role of the parent, preparing Natalie for the time when she would have a totally dependent infant.

Dreaming that you are pregnant may indicate a desire for a child, but it may also represent a new beginning or a creative development elsewhere in your life.

Nurturing a baby

Dreams of nurturing babies may be the precursor to initiating new projects; if the babies are happy it augurs well for success. It is useful to bear in mind that babies are fragile and need protection and tender loving care, so this dream may be reminding you that your new ideas should be treated as carefully as a newborn baby. The dream baby may also represent a newly emerging part of yourself, so treat yourself tenderly and ensure you look after your own well-being.

Forgetting about a baby

Quite often I dream that I have had a baby but have forgotten about it and am frantically searching for it or trying to get home to it.

LOUISA

If you ignore your deepest needs, emotional or spiritual, it is as irresponsible as taking on the care of a baby, then losing or forgetting it. In dreams where this happens consider what part of yourself you are forgetting to take care of. Also, look at how well you are cared for by others; such dreams may indicate that you need more nurturing from those around you.

Conceiving a baby

Women frequently dream of babies at ovulation when they are ready for conception. However, if they wish to conceive but are finding it difficult, they may have wish-fulfilment dreams in which the longed-for child arrives. Many women who record their dreams find that there are characteristic changes at ovulation and just prior to menstruation, when dreams of violence and blood are common themes, as I found in research for my book *Women Dreaming*, which deals with this in greater detail.

ROLE REVERSAL

When her mother became ill, Miranda had a dream in which her mother had shrunk to the size of a six-month-old baby and she had to take care of her. Symbolically, the dream shows how the mother-child role has reversed, a common experience for those with aged or infirm parents.

Dreaming about caring for a baby may indicate concern for a vulnerable person of any age.

BIRDS

Dreams of birds in flight
are frequently linked to our desire
to escape the earth's gravity that pulls us down literally and metaphorically. Birds are associated with the higher self, our spiritual side that soars from the earthly plane to the infinite heaven above. Like angels, they can indicate transcendence. Birds can also represent high-flying ambition and success. If you dream about a bird that is unable to fly, this can mean you feel frustrated with life and its pressures. A bird in a cage is an extreme example.

The specific type of creature is important, and its role in the dream sets the scene.

Cuckoo

A cuckoo may be a sign that there is a stranger in your midst who is trying to oust you. Cuckoos lay their eggs in other birds' nests. They don't build their own homes but muscle into other birds' territory and destroy the eggs and chicks of the host bird to ensure their own survival. Does this have echoes with any person in your life at present?

Dove

The dove signifies peace and love, as well as being a symbol of hope.

Eagle

The eagle is especially sacred to many Native American tribes, and its feathers were used in ceremonies, healing rituals, and placed around the body of a dead person to guide him or her heavenward. Ancient Aztecs believed the souls of dead warriors were transformed into eagles, which then went to guard the sun.

Hawk

A hawk is a bird of prey with supreme powers of vision and strength. If you dream of a hawk, are you on the look out or about to attack?

Owl

The wisdom of the owl is legendary; this bird also symbolizes transformation. In Hal's dream it forced him to face his previous lack of wisdom and plan radical changes in his life (see below).

Peacock

The peacock has the capacity to renew its brilliant plumage each year, and for this reason it became a Christian symbol for the resurrection. It is also known for its pride, so if you dream of a peacock, are you feeling "as proud as a peacock?"

Phoenix

This mythical bird, said to set fire to itself and rise from the ashes, represents renewal and a fresh start. It can also symbolize resurrection of an idea or situation, as well as longevity, and the indestructibility of the human spirit. A phoenix can also indicate beauty and quality.

HAL'S DREAM

I have twin brothers, and both are in prison awaiting trial for robbery. When I visited Hal the other day, he was talking about a dream he'd had that worried him. He said an owl had flown into his room and had kept flying around him.

THE BODY

Whenever your body has a significant impact in a dream, consider all its aspects; try to understand its direct and indirect meaning. Look at the message that may be carried by dreaming about specific parts of the body.

A skeleton in your dream may give the "bare bones," the essence of the matter that is of concern. The spine—symbolizing strength and support—can be a sign of courage; it could also stand for its opposite—someone who has "no backbone" and is showing weakness.

Your legs and feet connect you to the earth; they "ground" you and carry the rest of your body. If you feel your legs have "given way," does it mean that you don't feel able to carry the burden or have no support? If your foundation goes, as at

Head: a decision or conclusion is imminent

Arm: strong arms can indicate action and productivity

Spine: symbolizes courage and support. A lack of spine would mean weakness.

Feet: can indicate steadiness and confidence, or insecurity

Dreaming about a specific part of your body may indicate illness, or a more subtle meaning, as noted above.

a time of crisis or radical change, you may have "no leg to stand on," and may feel vulnerable.

Breasts are connected to mother's milk, life-giving sustenance, the earliest form of pure nourishment, and comfort.

If you dream of a head, it may mean that matters are coming to a head. The heads in John's dream held a particular meaning for him:

I walk into a room where there is a cupboard. When I open it there are shelves with people's heads lined up. I recognize some of them but can't put names to all of them. I see a space and it is marked for my head. When I see this I wake up. I call it my "Cupboard Full of Heads Dream."

To his wife and colleagues John appears happy and contented, but the severed heads indicate detachment and that he is hiding away his thoughts, and is unable to face them.

Our face is what we present to the world; it is our mask, our persona. Dreaming about putting on a "brave face" may mean you hide distress and feel cut off from love and support, in much the same way as the British "stiff upper lip" signifies the repression of hurt feelings.

Hair is an important sexual symbol for both sexes. Baldness represents losing potency, being exposed and vulnerable, being "bare" with no natural protection from the elements, no covering.

Loss of blood equals loss of strength. If you dream of losing blood, does it mean that your vital life force is seeping away? Are you being "drained" of vitality? Blood may also symbolize sacrifice. "When blood is spilled, battle is over" is an old saying. If blood figures in your dream it may mean that struggles are finally at an end.

Food and drink

What are you taking into your body? The type and quality of the food in your dream is significant. Is it nourishing and easily digested or is it "junk," which is ultimately unhealthy?

Prisoners deprived of food often dream of banquets, while slimmers dream of their favorite calorie-rich food and wake up feeling guilty, believing they really did eat the forbidden food. If you are hungry in a dream, is the hunger a symbolic sign that you are lacking something important—love, affection, or care, for instance ?

Slimmers often dream about calorie-rich food when they feel deprived. Dreaming about food can also indicate you lack love or affection.

Lavatories

This is a common theme in dreams. While a person is asleep the brain sometimes receives signals from the bladder that it needs to be emptied. The frustration of not finding a suitable lavatory may finally force the dreamer awake, as in Rosie's dream: "I have dreams all about desperate hunts for lavatories, which always turn out to be locked, blocked, or otherwise unusable. Eventually, I wake up dying to go to the bathroom, which has been incorporated into my dream."

Such dreams can also symbolize frustration, reflecting dissatisfaction with a waking situation that you want to eliminate or expel.

Clothes

In dreams, the way people are dressed gives important clues that help in dream interpretation. The self we present to the world is very much tied into the image we wish to project. The outside persona may be very different from the person underneath, but in order to conform to society's rules people tacitly agree to abide by a dress code, though in certain organizations and schools there will be an enforced code to which everyone has to adhere.

Exposure

Dreams in which clothing, or lack of it, leaves the dreamer exposed to public gaze may indicate feelings of helplessness and vulnerability. Vita had a recurring dream during a time of severe strain in her marriage:

Walking through the streets clothed in nightwear is a common dream, usually indicating vulnerability and fear of embarrassment.

I set off from home early in the morning and, miles away from home, I discover that I am in my nightgown and slippers. I try to rush back before too many people see me, but as I get nearer and nearer, there are more and more people who notice me and stare.

Vita lived in a small town, her husband's affairs were known to everyone before she finally discovered his infidelity. Her dreams clearly express vulnerability and exposure in the public arena.

Dreams of being in a public place with an undershirt that is too short or underpants that are too scanty are related to feelings of being exposed or vulnerable. Perhaps you have been too revealing about personal information, showing the layers below the social façade we commonly use to protect our deeper selves. When clothes are stripped away, it is the secret self that is revealed and this may cause discomfort. Such dreams are helpful; you can use them to check out whether you are being too trusting with people who might take advantage of your revelations.

Caiti has had a recurring dream that was worrying for her:

I have a short time to get to an appointment and find myself undressed and searching for clothes—the rows of dresses are all forgotten ones that seem to have something wrong with them when I put them on or I am searching through a pile of pantyhose and none of them are fit to wear.

Uniforms

Uniforms project a corporate image and give a unified persona or front. A uniform in a dream may represent the symbolic qualities associated with that particular uniform, for example, the protection of the police, the power of prison guards, the authority of a supreme court judge.

CLOTHING WORD PLAY

In dreams a particular article of clothing may serve as a code or symbol for something you are having difficulty facing directly. So when examining your dreams, don't forget the word play or puns behind the clothing. Here are some examples:

• **A dress:** an address you live at, or is someone addressing their remarks to you?

• **Cloak:** does this symbolize secrecy, cover-up, or protection?

• **Suit:** does this represent suitability?

• **Sneakers:** is this simple footwear, or is someone or something sneaking up on you?

DEATH

In antiquity, Hypnos—the god of sleep—and Thanatos—the god of death—were looked on as divine brothers, which probably gave us the saying that sleep is the "little death." In fairy tales in many cultures, sleep is the world of the repressed, dormant side, the submerged aspect of the self that is waiting to be released at the right moment.

Although dreams of death can be very disturbing, they are not necessarily connected to physical death. Traumatic and serious life changes may trigger such dreams, signifying the end of one part of life and the beginning of another. These dreams are commonly experienced at times of separation and divorce. Dreams of death can help to prepare you for a new beginning as you let go of your past lifestyle.

Annihilation

I was in a fight and was almost being strangled. I was scared, frightened of being dead, of being no more. Not being able to hear my own heart beat.

ANTON

Whereas death can be viewed as part of the cycle of life and may indicate a new, positive start, annihilation means total destruction. A sense of being annihilated can be terrifying and an important indication that there is a serious internal or external conflict in the dreamer's life. Anton could ask himself what part of his self is being so "cut off" or choked back that it stops his heart from beating.

Dreaming about death can be disturbing, but it can also have a positive meaning, such as signifying the end of a particular cycle in order to make way for a new beginning.

Impending death

People who are close to death, or who have a member of their immediate family in this situation, often dream of relatives who have already died. They come as companions, as escorts to the afterlife, and offer much comfort. This is probably where the term "Angel of Death" comes from. Sometimes we dream of those we love who are terminally ill, as Dawn did:

DAWN'S DREAM

I felt that a dream I had about many mice foretold a death. It was a dark room, with lagged pipes and stacks of dirty clothes. There was a figure in the corner shrouded in white cloth. The mice in the room did not go near the figure though they were seething everywhere. I was horrified, though in waking life I am not afraid of mice. I saw the dream as a death. My brother was ill with cancer at the time. The pipes seemed to be blood vessels. The dream prepared me a little bit.

Dreams of mice and rats often indicate that something or someone in the dreamer's life is worn out by the gnawing "tooth of time" and is about to disappear, which was the case for Dawn. Dreams of death may teach us how to

die, or how to let those we love release their earthly connections, as Dawn's dream did.

Dreaming of the dead

Dreams of those who are dead are part of the grieving process. Feelings of guilt, anger, or sadness may surface and recurring dreams indicate the need to complete some "unfinished business" concerning the deceased. Perhaps there was something you needed to say? Did a longed-for reconciliation not take place? Face whatever uncomfortable emotions are stirred up and work on your dreams as part of the process of grieving and renewal.

Dreams about impending death can take many forms. The appearance of an angel or deceased relative can offer comfort.

Dreams about mice or rats often indicate time is passing for someone.

39

Falling is a very common dream. It is usually associated with a fear or failure.

You may receive a subliminal piece of information about an unguarded area in your home, such as a balcony or dangerous flooring.

Loss of control

Our language has many examples in which falling is associated with loss of control: the unexpected removal of a dependable object—having "the rug pulled from under us"—causes us to fall; we "fall in love" as if out of control; we "fall for it," when duped by a conman. So dreams of falling may indicate a lack of control in your life.

Letting go

If you have a dream in which you are falling, ask yourself what it is you fear. Falling from grace, losing esteem in other people's eyes, sliding down the hierarchy at work? Perhaps part of you wants to give up control and to "let go." Or as Bernie Siegel, well-known author of *Love, Medicine and Miracles*, says, "Let go, and let God." Accepting that you cannot control everything can be a liberating experience.

FALLING

Falling dreams are very common at times of instability. When we lose the ground, when "the ground gives way beneath us," we lose stability. Falling is also associated with failure, or fear of failure, and may indicate a fear that you will not achieve your goal. However, always check the setting of a dream in which a fall occurs; it could be a practical warning about a potential danger.

Landing in a field of clover or other soft surface marks a transition point in your life.

Point of impact

Falling in dreams is an unpleasant sensation but, despite superstitious beliefs, if you hit the ground in a falling dream it does not mean you will die. I have been asked this on many occasions and can assure you that this superstition is untrue; I've met many people who have lived to tell me about the impact! Indeed, the point of impact is often a point of transition. The hard earth turns into a mattress of clover, or a road becomes a river in which the dreamer floats.

The mythological fall

Common to mythologies around the world is the theme of "the fall" or the loss of connection to the divine. In Christianity, Adam and Eve were expelled from the Garden of Eden, and this "fall" from paradise is linked to the loss of godlike immortality and humanity's independence.

FIRE

Throughout history, fire and the sun have been regarded as sacred. It is a symbol of transformation and purification. With lighted candles we invoke divine intervention; the flame burns in perpetuity for the unknown soldier; the fires of the funeral pyres and cremations transform bodies, freeing the soul from bodily constraints; the fire that burns in the hearth has always been the symbolic center of the home.

In dreams, fire is a sign of powerful natural energy. It relates to our power to generate energy in some form, be it flares of anger, smoldering rage, or bursts of brilliance. Fire also illuminates, so a dream fire in the form of torches, beacons, intense sunshine, and glowing lamps could symbolize enlightenment and a new start.

Fire as a warning

With fire, there always is a sinister undercurrent: we know it is dangerous to play with fire. Fire can get out of control, become all-engulfing and destroy anything in its path. So if fire appears in your dream, ask yourself how you felt about it? Were you warmed by the heat or roasted? Was the fire all-consuming? Is there some aspect of your life that is too hot to handle?

Fire can symbolize enlightenment, and combined with a strong, confident figure can mean a momentous revelation.

FLYING

Flying makes a regular appearance in childhood dreams. Children often see themselves flying downstairs, out through bedroom windows, and over cityscapes. These dreams survive into adulthood and remain a common theme. In some instances dreams of flying precede out-of-body experiences and lucid dreams, which are explored on pages 114–116.

Flying rarely has a sexual meaning, as popularly believed. It usually signifies ambition and a desire to overcome the mundane.

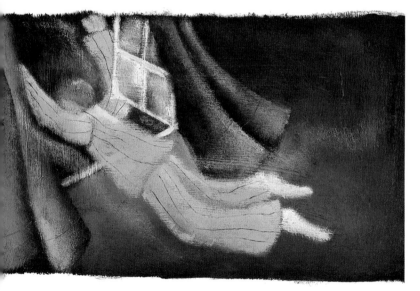

Power

Flying dreams are typically associated with power, giving dreamers the chance to soar, to climb above the mundane for a clearer view; they give access to another element, the air, where restrictions fall away. If something wonderful happens to you and you feel exhilarated, you may have dreams of gliding effortlessly in heavenly spheres, high above the stuff of everyday life.

Fear

Often it is fear that triggers off a flying dream; the dreamer needs to rise above danger in order to escape. In Chloe's flying dream, she metaphorically removes herself from a dangerous situation, which will have a parallel in daily life:

I dream a lot about flying. These are usually nightmares where I am trying to escape. Someone evil is trying to get me so I run and flap my arms. Sometimes I get just a couple of inches off the ground, other times I get about six feet high but I can never stay up in the air. I struggle to fly the most whenever the frightening thing is really close. I have never been caught.

Anita also had dreams of flying from danger:

I could change into a butterfly and fly off to safety whenever I felt threatened.

High fliers

Flying dreams may reveal your ambition to be a "high flier," to reach the top in your chosen field, perhaps at work or in sports. Do you need to have a high profile, to be up there for everyone to see?

Spiritual aspirations

Flight may also represent spiritual development, spiritual aspirations, and a desire for transcendence. Birds and angels have wings to take them heavenward and are viewed as intermediaries between the heavenly and earthly planes.

If an unusual flying creature appears in a dream, look at its prominent characteristics for significance.

Flying creatures

When flying creatures such as birds, bats, and insects appear in your dreams, look at their individual characteristics to understand their significance. The bat flies blind, trusting its sonar skills to avoid danger. Are you metaphorically flying blind, or is your dream telling you that you have other senses you can develop? Look at the section on birds for more information on the symbolism of flying creatures.

HOUSES

Houses frequently represent the body and/or personality of the dreamer. The outside of the building symbolizes the outer persona, the front we show to the external world; the interior relates to feelings and the internal workings of the body. Each floor of the building has a particular significance: the top floors reflect what is happening in the head and mind; the cellars or basement link to the unconscious and our instincts, which are usually below the surface and kept in the dark. Ceilings represent protection or limitation, perhaps the "glass ceiling" that some women experience when attempting to fulfil career ambitions.

State of repair

The state of repair of the dream house or building is important. Is it well maintained, or is it neglected? Walls offer protection or provide boundaries, so if these are crumbling, you may need to become clear about what you find acceptable in your relationships with other people and where you draw the boundaries between your needs and theirs.

Breaking in

If your house is under attack or if someone is trying to break in, does this express concerns about personal safety or fears about an unhappy or undermining relationship?

> *When I'm stressed I dream about people throwing rocks through the window, breaking it. Then I hide under the table hoping they won't get me.*
>
> DWIGHT

A broken window may reveal concerns about personal safety or a destructive relationship. Do you feel under attack?

Doors, windows, and keys

The openings to buildings—for example doors and windows—may symbolize orifices in the body such as the eyes or mouth. When doors are closed to you or windows so dirty that you cannot see through them, ask yourself what you are locking away or refusing to see. Keys, for doors or windows, can give access to understanding, the ability to solve difficulties or to unlock knowledge.

Rooms

Each individual room in the house has its own symbolic significance for the dreamer. The bathroom is the place of cleansing and elimination. The bedroom is an area of privacy, retreat, and rest, as well as intimacy. The kitchen is the heart of the home, center of nourishment. The cellar and the foundations represent the deepest aspect of your unconscious. Halls and corridors are passages that connect, that link one aspect to another; they are places of transition.

Stairs

Some dream theorists say that climbing stairs symbolizes the male erection, while descending them symbolizes detumescence after orgasm. Others believe that climbing stairs relates to ambition and rising status at work or in personal

Stairs and staircases can mean many things. Asking yourself how you cope with the stairs can be very revealing.

A new room in your dream may be a sign that it is time for you to begin a new venture. The kind of room it is may throw light on which path to follow.

The language of symbols

relationships. Once again the important thing is to ask yourself how your dream stairs relate to your waking life. Are you going up or down? Are you reaching new heights but scared of climbing the stairs? Is it easy to climb the stairs?

New rooms

When you begin a new project, or are about to do so, you may discover new rooms in your dreams, which indicates that you are ready to develop a new venture. These may be rooms that have previously been closed to you, as in Annie's dream:

ANNIE'S DREAM

My recurring dream is that I discover a wing or rooms in a house. More often than not, these "surprise" rooms are furnished with old furniture and when I look in the drawers I find them full of different items, from treasure to chocolate. I am always delighted to find these rooms.

JOURNEYS

Traveling in dreams can give you important clues about your life path and your sense of personal fulfilment. When you undertake a journey, the destination, the means of transportation, your traveling companions, and the route, all reveal your physical, emotional, and spiritual state.

If you make a record of your traveling dreams, you may find that you are repeatedly given sweet things along the way, such as jars of honey, cakes, or sweet fruit. Such sweetness affirms the pleasures available to you should you undertake a voyage of discovery. Conversely, if your travel dreams are full of adversity and frustration, perhaps you have taken a wrong turning and need to consider where you are going in your life.

Frustrated at every turn

Being delayed, missing trains, not knowing what you are supposed to be doing or where you are going are typical anxiety themes. If you have this type of dream, you may feel panic and wake up breathless and covered in perspiration.

If you dream of being held back or hindered by people or circumstances, try making connections from the clues your dreams give. For instance, is

Making connections between the clues in your dreams can help you piece together the "dream jigsaw" and gain valuable insights into the circumstances surrounding you. This information will enable you to improve the quality of your life and your well-being.

someone blocking your path? Are you in a testing situation such as a job interview? Did you notice a "dead end" sign, but chose to ignore it? Examine all the elements of the dream jigsaw to get the full picture.

LEILA'S DREAM

I have a recurring dream of being on a journey, but I don't know where I'm supposed to be going. I lose my way, lose my belongings, and I don't know which train to take. I never get to my destination.

Stops en route

On your dream journey, be it by car, on foot, or by plane, you may find yourself making stops en route. These stops allow you to make decisions about the journey, to rest, to take in nourishing food to sustain you on the trip; they are places where you may find new information about your destination or destiny. Pay particular attention to these stopping-off places and the people you meet there. What is being offered to you? Will it be of value, will it help you fulfil your destiny?

FEAR OF FLYING

Fear of flying is a debilitating phobia that can ruin plans for long-distance travel. Joanna, who lived in Dublin, longed to go to Los Angeles for a vacation, but having suffered travel sickness since childhood, she dreaded the journey and, in particular, was terrified of flying. Throwing caution to the winds she booked a ticket and hoped for the best:

About six weeks before the departure date I knew I would have to come to terms with this fear. I had several dreams that started with me actually being in the United States, where I had never been, and the dreams showed I would fly there with no fear and enjoy my stay.

When she woke, Joanna wondered why she had not dreamed of the long journey and believed her dreams held a message: "The flying aspect shouldn't be on your mind, so let's get on with the vacation." As a consequence of these dreams, she found that her attitude toward flying changed and she flew to Los Angeles with complete confidence. She has planned a second trip this year!

Dreaming about travel may help you cope with a fear of flying.

A complicated, dense maze indicates difficulty and confusion in life. Escaping the maze means you are ready to solve a problem.

LABYRINTHS AND MAZES

The labyrinth or maze is sometimes seen as a symbol of difficulty or confusion, expressing the trials and tribulations of life. If you find yourself in a labyrinth, perhaps you are faced with a situation of such complexity that you don't know how to get through it or where to turn next.

A maze usually has several dead-end passages. If a maze appears in your dreams, it usually indicates that there is a puzzle or problem that you are faced with. If you are lost in a maze or labyrinth, uncertainty and indecision about your next course of action may be holding you back. If you are finding your way out of a maze or labyrinth, or leading someone else out, then you have almost certainly resolved, or are about to resolve, whatever difficulty was in your path.

You may dream of a labyrinth or maze when you think you have exhausted all possible ways to resolve a difficult situation. You feel you have come to a "dead-end." Every object, plant, or item

THE LABYRINTH AND THE MINOTAUR

According to legend, a labyrinth was built in ancient Crete to contain the minotaur, a monster that was half man and half bull. Every nine years, seven young boys and seven maidens were sent into the labyrinth to be devoured by the minotaur. Eventually, Theseus was sent in to kill the beast and managed to do so with the help of his lover Ariadne. She gave him a ball of golden thread to unwind as he entered the labyrinth, and by using her thread to keep track of his journey, he was able to find his way out after he had killed the minotaur. The golden thread that saved Theseus symbolizes divine instinct and intuitive power; killing the beast symbolizes our ability to overcome our animalistic, base nature.

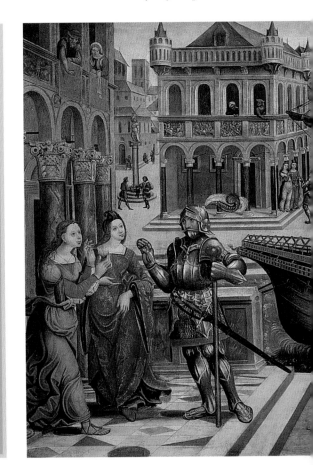

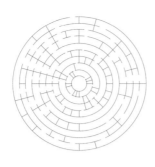

you encounter in the dream maze will provide a clue to help you find your way out. For instance, you may find that a plant in the maze is labeled "Rue," which is for remembrance. What do you need to remember that will help you out of your current difficulties?

A labyrinth can also be the path that leads to deeper knowledge and understanding. The symbol of the labyrinth appears in ancient Egypt, in Celtic mythology, as well as in Tibetan and Indian cultures. In most cases it represents the inner journey that each of us must make through conflict and confusion to discover our true nature, which lies at the center of our being.

A dream of an archetypal, circular labyrinth may indicate that you are on the journey from pure physicality to spiritual enlightenment. In many places today, including Grace Cathedral in San Francisco and Saffron Walden Common in Essex, England, you can walk through a labyrinth as part of a waking journey of spiritual transformation and inner healing.

Labyrinths and mazes are archetypal symbols and have been used to symbolize confusion and adventure for many centuries.

Dreaming about loss, such as a kidnap or becoming lost, is common for the bereaved.

LOSS

If you have suffered a bereavement or separation from someone you love, you are likely to find that your dreams reverberate with themes of loss, such as kidnap, amputation, disintegration, losing things, and becoming lost.

Losing things

When you lose something in a dream, the symbolic nature of the item will give you a clue to the dream's meaning. For instance, if you lose a purse or wallet with credit cards, driver's license, and other personal items, it may indicate that you feel disempowered or have lost your creditable standing with other people. Have you lost your confidence or your sense of identity? If you lose a watch, are you losing or wasting time? Has the watch gone because you are not being watchful? If so, the dream is advising you to be more vigilant about a situation you are involved in.

Losing a wallet or purse may indicate that you have lost your confidence.

At a loss

At times everything that is familiar takes on a different hue, and seems strange and unknown. If this happens in your dreams, ask yourself if you are taking your life and those around you for granted; perhaps there are changes that you have failed to notice. Use the dream prompt to see if there are other ways of looking at familiar situations to give you new insights.

LOST ON A JOURNEY

When you are lost on a journey it may mean that you have started off from the wrong place or missed an important landmark along the way. This type of dream may be a metaphor for making the wrong decision—taking the wrong turning, losing your way, or missing an opportunity. Terri had a recurring dream of being lost:

My recurring dream occurs after particular periods of stress and involves being lost or not being able to find my way along streets that are all the same. I am usually heading for home or somewhere that during the day I could find my way to blindfolded. However, in my dreams the streets are all strange. The stores have all changed hands, as if I had been picked up and put down in a city on the other side of the mirror—a looking-glass city, in fact. Very weird! But I seem to realize what is happening and often say to myself "it's only a dream," while I am actually dreaming.

Circumstances in Terri's life may have forced her to go along a path she regrets. If you have this type of dream, ask yourself what you can do to discover the route in life that is best for you now. Ask your dreams to show you the "right way" and then set about making some positive changes.

MARRIAGE

Dreams of marriage, of symbolic union and completion, are particularly prevalent when love blooms. When you fall in love, nothing else feels as important as the person you love, and obviously your dreams will reflect your waking obsession.

In symbolic terms, a marriage is the joining together of opposites to bring about completion; it can therefore represent a mystical union or conjunction. If you dream of a marriage but have no plans to marry, or you are already married, ask yourself whether you are joining together different parts of your life, putting together two things that have previously been separate. It may even be about your professional or political "union."

Wedding rings can symbolize a new and lasting commitment. Wearing a wedding ring can also symbolize a loss of independence and a fear of responsibility.

a new social status. It can also symbolize the loss of independence and the taking on of new, challenging responsibilities.

The wedding cake

Similarly, the wedding cake, the "breaking of bread" (or cake) by the two partners and their families, represents union. If you dream of such a cake, it may symbolize the richness and sweetness of your relationship. If the cake has many layers, it could be interpreted as a status symbol.

The wedding ring

A wedding ring symbolizes eternity; it has no beginning or end. If you dream of a wedding ring being placed on your finger, it signifies a new commitment and

Confetti, and other traditional wedding motifs, could signify a romantic, professional or political "union."

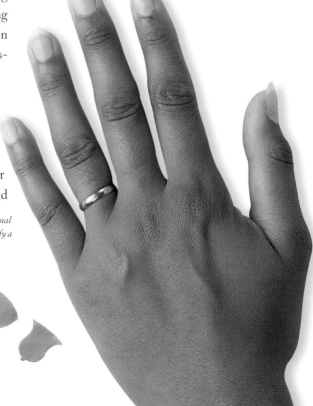

Partners often share similar dreams, with shared hopes and fears.

DREAM LOVERS

Very often lovers have the same or very similar dreams, or each partner dreams of the other person. The bond between them is so strong that even in their sleeping state they share their lives.

Sometimes, even when lovers are separated by long distances, they can still communicate with each other through their dreams. Talk to your lover about your dreams, share your experiences, and you may find that whatever is of mutual importance appears in your dreams.

KIRSTY'S DREAM

I have once or twice dreamed that I am about to be married to someone I did not know or like and that it was too late to back out.

Unwanted marriage

Dreams of unwanted marriages may be telling you that a partner is unsuitable for you or that you do not really want to marry, even though all the preparations have been made. Such a dream may also be warning you that all is not as it appears to be. It can also refer to other situations, for example unease about a job opportunity or a potential business partnership.

MONSTERS

Nightmares featuring monsters are one of the most common dreams, particularly with young children. They can be extremely upsetting, and can disturb sleep patterns.

Worry and anxiety are likely to trigger recurring monster dreams. They may follow a pattern or adopt various guises, but these dreams will repeat themselves until you respond to their message. When you face monsters in your dreams, try to figure out what or who they represent and why they are chasing or attacking you. Do they symbolize a fear or sense of threat that bothers you during the day? Monsters can represent the shadow side of yourself or relate to someone you are afraid of in waking life. Keeping a detailed record of dreams will help you to appreciate your monster's attempts to communicate.

Confront and conquer

I occasionally have a nightmare about the sudden appearance of a man/monster. This actually makes my spine chill. I always wake up as soon as he appears and it is some time before I can get back to sleep.

TIM

Tim escapes his pursuer by waking, a common escape mechanism, but next time he has the nightmare he could try to turn and face the man/monster and ask him what he wants. This strategy, known as "confront and conquer," often prevents a recurrence of the nightmare.

When you are chased by a monster in your dream, make an effort to turn and face it. Look at it and identify what it is that threatens you. Very often the act of facing our fears enables us to find a way of overcoming them. Persuade your monster to speak to you. Ask why it is pursuing you and try to find out what it wants from you.

If you cannot confront and conquer your monster while dreaming, when you wake try the dream dialogue technique (see page 21). This is a very helpful way to clarify what the monster represents and what aspect of your life it symbolizes. Once you understand the reason for its presence, the greater is the likelihood that you can eradicate it.

A dream "monster" can take many forms. The common factor in all monster dreams is a feeling of threat and danger.

Goya's persecution by evil creatures in his dreams inspired him to create his famous painting The Sleep of Reason Produces Monsters.

The incubus attack

The most vivid dream I ever had was about an evil force, which I believed to be the devil, and a great weight that was pressing down on my stomach and I could not speak or shout. The most frightening thing about that dream was that I find it difficult to come to terms with the fact that it was a dream because to me at the time, it was actually happening and it occurred over and over again.

MATTIE

This kind of attack is sometimes known as the incubus attack and usually happens during the early part of non-REM sleep. The sensations of choking, suffocation, and a heavy weight on the chest along with a feeling of doom, are less to do with dreams than physiological changes in the body. They are a disturbance in the body's arousal system and not necessarily related to psychological trauma.

THE SLEEP OF REASON PRODUCES MONSTERS

Goya's painting *The Sleep of Reason Produces Monsters* arose from his waking worries. He was persecuted by dream demons in the shape of fiendish owls, predatory cats, and bats ready to swoop and devour him. Such night creatures symbolize our primitive fear of the evils that may be lurking in the dark of the night, or in the dark of the soul.

SLEEP PARALYSIS

In a terrifying dream monsters may force us to wake up so quickly that we are still caught in sleep paralysis. When we enter dream sleep, our muscles normally get "switched off" so that we don't start acting out those dreams of hitting people or running away. This safety mechanism is obviously useful but can be frightening when you suddenly wake up and cannot shout out or move your body. Try not to worry, just wait for your sleepy muscles to catch up with your waking mind.

The Moon is deeply significant in many cultures. Noting the shape of the moon will help with interpretation of your dream.

MOON

The moon is associated with sleep, darkness, and the feminine intuitive side. In alchemy, the moon was seen as the guardian of the dark occult powers, in contrast to the sun, which signified the physical, observable world.

In ancient times, the planting of crops was timed to coincide with certain lunar phases, so the moon became synonymous with fertility. In ancient Egypt, to see the moon in a dream was a favorable sign; it signified the female, maternal, and the all-forgiving mother.

The phases of the moon

The moon is constantly changing, and each lunar phase has symbolic significance to the dreamer. A new moon (a narrow waxing crescent) is a sign of rebirth, and may indicate a time for stillness and meditation. In Native American traditions, the women would retreat at this time in order to commune with the Great Spirit. It was an important time of reflection and preparation. A crescent moon that waxes, or grows larger, symbolizes a time of expansion and growth for the dreamer. A full moon represents a culmination of work and efforts. It can also signify pregnancy, or feeling maternal. A waning moon indicates a time to absorb all you have learned from the preceding weeks or a gradual decrease in power.

The ancient Greek moon goddess Selene gave her name to the stone selenite, which is excellent for aiding dream recall and dream interpretation. Place it close to your bed if you are having problems remembering your dreams.

NIGHTMARE IMAGES

My dreams set me up for the start of my day. If it is a good dream, I have a good day but if it's a nightmare, I have a bad day.

RICHARD

In nightmares we feel as if we are caught in an horrific situation that often involves being trapped, injured, or killed. The dreamer often wakes up shaking, breathing rapidly, crying, or feeling extremely anxious. It used to be thought that nightmares were visited upon the dreamer by

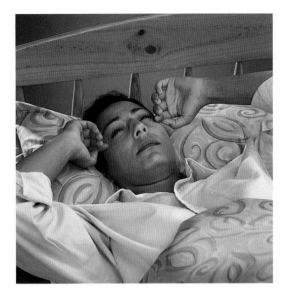

Nightmares can be triggered by worry, stress, or fear. The dreamer often wakes up feeling disturbed and anxious.

an outside force; in fact, the term nightmare means "night demon." Nowadays, we are more likely to see nightmares as the result of personal demons that must be recognized and dealt with. We realize that nightmares are sparked off by unhappy personal events, waking worries, feuds, and stress. People who commit acts of which they are ashamed or, at the extreme, criminal acts of assault or murder, are often plagued by nightmares. Like Macbeth, the deed haunts them as they sleep. There are other triggers for nightmares such as medication, alcohol, and high fever, as well as the pernicious influence of horror videos and violent movies.

Marie had a series of horrendous nightmares after the death of her husband :

They are all variations on a theme. I see Gary walking toward me but then his flesh starts to fall off and he turns into a skeleton.

Her nightmares vividly dramatize the illness and death of her husband, in which she watched him "waste away" before her eyes in the short weeks leading to his death.

THE INFLUENCE OF THE MOON

The moon controls the tides, including the monthly cycles of women. Our blood is 98 percent water, and our blood chemistry is very similar to sea water, so it is not surprising that we should be influenced by the phases of the moon just as the oceans are; tides flow within us both.

At the new moon and first quarter stage, I dream constantly. I wake up in the morning feeling as though I have been living a separate existence and have not slept at all.

DIANA

Shakespeare's Macbeth suffered nightmares and premonitions as a result of his actions.

ADOLF HITLER'S NIGHTMARE

In 1917, when Adolf Hitler was serving as a corporal in the Bavarian Infantry, he had a nightmare in which he was being buried under an avalanche of earth and molten iron. He woke up, desperately wanted some air and so left the dugout in which he had been sleeping. He felt impelled to get away from the trench even though he was in a war zone and was in danger of enemy gunfire. Suddenly he was brought to his senses when the enemy opened fire. He rushed back to his dugout only to find it had been completely obliterated along with all his comrades. A direct hit had made a crater and covered it with burning debris. From that moment on Hitler felt he had been given a divine mission and had only to wait to discover what it was. Sadly, it meant World War II and the eventual death of millions of people.

Night terrors (*pavor nocturnus*)

A night terror is actually a sleep disorder, though many sufferers describe it as a nightmare because they do not realize what is happening to them. Recent research shows that night terrors often run in families, and can occur in all age-groups. Night terrors usually occur during non-REM sleep rather than REM sleep, which is when dreams usually happen. Night terrors normally strike within an hour of going to sleep and may last between 5 and 20 minutes. Although the person is still asleep, the eyes are wide open, giving the impression that the dreamer is wide awake. This rarely happens during regular REM sleep. Though night terrors are particularly frightening for the observer, bear in mind that they are not inherently dangerous and, on waking, the person will only feel tired, and perhaps a little confused. The real threat occurs if the person sleepwalks and may get hurt.

The symptoms of night terrors are usually a sudden waking from sleep, a persistent fear or terror that comes on only at night, screaming, sweating, palpitations, confusion, inability to

TOMO'S DREAM

Helpful nightmares are often riddles and I think about them so much that all sorts of things get dredged up so that they indirectly illuminate dark corners.

explain what happened, and no recall of the "bad dream" or "nightmare" on waking. It can be very difficult to comfort a person who is experiencing a night terror, and prevention is better.

There has been some success in reducing or preventing night terrors. Done over a period of four days or so, this technique of interrupting the pattern of night terrors appears to disrupt the night terror routine (see below). If this does not work, seek help from a sleep disorder clinic.

A night terror may last between 5 and 20 minutes. During this time the dreamer may sleep with his or her eyes open.

PREVENTING NIGHT TERRORS

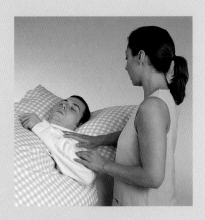

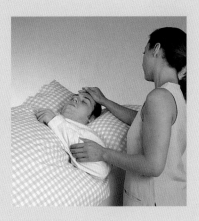

1 Monitor the time the person normally experiences a night terror, then over a period of time of three or four nights, wake him or her before the time of the anticipated attack.

2 Rouse the person sufficiently to be able to sit up and have a drink of water. Try to make this a quiet time with as little conversation as possible.

3 Help the person to become comfortable again, and leave him or her to get back to sleep. This method helps to disrupt a pattern of night terrors.

PREGNANCY

Dreams throughout pregnancy are often far more vivid than usual, largely because of the changes in hormone levels during this time. REM sleep is

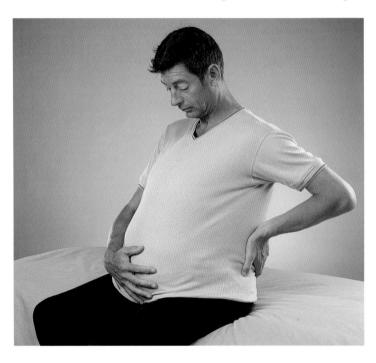

It is not unusual for men who have a pregnant partner to dream about being pregnant themselves. It demonstrates sympathy and preoccupation with impending parenthood.

extended so there is greater opportunity for more complex dreams, which often include sexually explicit events. However, not all dreams about becoming pregnant or being pregnant are about babies; they may be about the development of new aspects of yourself or new ventures in your life. Men may dream of being pregnant, either in the symbolic sense of new creative potential or in sympathy with a pregnant partner. Similarly, dreams about birth may represent the actual birth of a baby or symbolize the arrival of new ideas, fresh prospects, and increased potential.

FEAR OF PREGNANCY

Pregnancy dreams may prompt wise self-protection at times when you are being less than careful or not thinking clearly. Rosie's dreams about babies acted as a warning:

When I was about 16 and started having regular sexual intercourse, I was terrified of getting pregnant. I would sometimes dream that I was pregnant and my parents went crazy and my dad hit my boyfriend. In waking life it was a great relief not to be pregnant. These dreams made me even more wary of the consequences and therefore I decided to take precautions and started taking oral contraceptive pills.

Dreaming about having an unwanted pregnancy can remind you to take precautions.

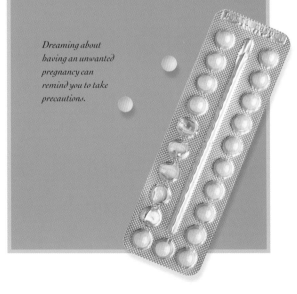

KAREN'S DREAM

Karen had this very realistic dream when she was just 12 days into her first pregnancy:

By the power of thought I was moving egg-shaped objects across a room. I was moving a plastic bag of olives and a beautiful gemstone. I felt that the bag held a deformed thing, something like a monkey.

Karen had just had a pregnancy test and said that part of her was terrified of producing an awful freak. The gemstone symbolizes the fragility and beauty of the embryo; the bag the embryonic sac; and the monkey the primitive life form.

Fertility symbols

There are many fertility symbols that appear in dreams, such as the phallic maypole of English tradition, newly plowed fields, seeds, and eggs. Fish symbolize fertility and abundance because they lay so many eggs. The frog, because of its great fecundity, was the symbol of Heket, the Egyptian goddess of birth. Water imagery is also linked with conception and birth.

CARMEN'S DREAM

Carmen's dream in the latter stages of pregnancy was a joyous introduction to her unborn son:

In it my child appeared as a tiny, delicate, skinny, black-haired mite, fragile and extraordinarily beautiful. He was so lovely in this dream that it felt to be one of the happiest dreams I have ever experienced and my baby was exactly like him.

The dream was so suffused with love that Carmen bonded with her child before she ever set eyes on him, and it set the tone for a strong, loving relationship that continues today.

A fish is a fertility symbol and may symbolize pregnancy or a new start.

Eggs are potent fertility symbols. A cracked egg symbolizes fragility, and may be a health warning.

RELATIONSHIPS

Relationships are a regular feature of our dream world: relationships with friends, family, lovers, neighbors, colleagues, and those who have left for another place or another person. These dreams may offer new understanding about the way you relate to others and how they relate to each other.

Dreaming about a person has changed my opinion of him or her. For example, if I have a dream where I am "in love" with a man, it does make me feel more positively toward him, almost as if I know him better. That person also feels more important to me if he knows that he features in my dreams. Whenever I talk to a person about the dream I give a "censored" version.

NICOLE

Dreaming about meeting a new lover may be a wish fulfilment, or it may be telling you something about an existing relationship or how you relate to an important person in your life.

Dream lover

Your dream lover may be someone you know, or a complete stranger. Some people have dreamed of an unknown lover, whom they have eventually met in their waking world. This could be a result of the sleeping mind identifying what you find attractive. Record your dreams so that you can check out whether this happens to you.

SARA'S DREAM

Sometimes I can wake up from a very vivid dream in which I feel deeply in love and really believe it happened. It puts me in a good mood for the rest of the day.

Trapped in a relationship

Claustrophobic and unhappy relationships often lead to dreams in which the dreamer is trapped, isolated, stuck on an island, or imprisoned. If you have such dreams, ask yourself if a significant relationship, at home or at work, is hampering you. Is there anything else in the dream that may provide a clue? Such dreams bring to consciousness truths that are denied in waking hours.

We often dream about complex emotional issues by projecting our thoughts onto objects. A turbulent sea, for example, may indicate anger or loss of control.

HELEN'S DREAM

I once had a dream of being trapped in a box and the sides started to close in on me. I had similar dreams a number of times and when I tried to read into it, I knew I felt trapped in a real life relationship—I thought he was tying me down. I got out of the relationship—that dream did me a lot of good.

Record any dialogue you have in your dreams. This can offer fascinating insights into your relationships.

Projections

Our feelings about relationships can be complex and confused. Research has shown that we try to make sense of relationships during dreams by projecting our feelings onto people or objects.

Usually, the positive projections are onto people close to us: a loving partner, a gentle friend, and so on; the more negative projections are usually on people farther away from us. It is always worth checking if the emotion expressed in a dream is one that you feel but have some difficulty expressing.

Anger in dreams can be a form of projection. Subconsciously you are afraid to reveal your emotions so you project them onto someone else. The raging woman in your dream may in fact represent your own fury, which is too uncomfortable to acknowledge when you are awake.

The projections may be onto objects too: a stormy sea may reveal personal energy or passion that is out of control; an ice-covered lake may appear when you feel emotionally frozen or neglected; a tiny mouse may represent your timidity and feelings of insignificance.

Isolation

My dreams are all about being locked out or not being able to let anyone know that I've arrived.

CHRISTINE

This feeling of being lost, and the sense of isolation, stems from Christine's experience as a child. Her father died when she was six and she was uprooted from her home in Canada. In many ways she still feels "locked out" from relationships because of that early trauma of loss.

A recurring dream may reveal that you are unable to cope with an important issue. Reliving a conversation or event while you are asleep can be a useful way of working through it.

The end of a relationship

I have a recurring dream, about once a week, of being chased by my ex-husband. I run up a gravel path, then fall. I desperately need someone to help me up. I panic because no one is there.

PIPPA

Dreams play out unfinished business even after a relationship has officially ended. Your mind may relive past events and conversations, and this can be emotionally draining. In Pippa's dream, the stalking fear that lingers from an abusive marriage manifests itself and shows her that she needs to gain support to get over her pain.

RITES OF PASSAGE

A rite of passage is a special point in life when there is a change in a person's status, for instance, when a child reaches adulthood, or when a single person gets married. Sometimes the point of transition is marked by a special ceremony such as a baptism in the Christian tradition or the bar mitzvah in the

Dreaming about baptism may symbolize a new opportunity or a fresh start.

One of the most meaningful rites of passage, a wedding can symbolize many things to a dreamer.

united with nurturing people, a joining of opposites, or finding balance. See also the Marriage entry on page 52.

Funeral
Funeral are about endings, throwing off outworn values and behavior, and letting go of the past.

Examinations
If you dream you are writing an exam or your knowledge or skills are being tested in some way, it may mean that you need to show your capability, that you must prove yourself. Perhaps you feel you are being scrutinized before you move to a higher position.

Jewish tradition. Even if important changes are not always marked by outward ceremony, they may appear symbolically in dreams. If you dream of any of the following rites of passage, but you are not actively involved in such an event in your waking life, try to discover what it means on a symbolic level.

Baptism
In baptism, there is a symbolic washing away of sin, a purification that signifies a new life of some kind for the dreamer, often involving a new identity. This is usually accompanied by being given a new name. The baptismal font is often eight-sided because eight is the number of regeneration. When you dream of baptism, it may represent a new aspect of yourself or a fresh start; it could also signify a change of outlook, or forgiveness.

Marriage
A dream that features a marriage may be telling you something about union, finding a kindred spirit, being

INITIATION RITES

In many religions and cults, dreams have been used to show when would-be religious aspirants are ready for initiation. In the cult of the Goddess Isis, both the initiate and the priest had to dream of the goddess at the same time. This was the sign that the initiation could proceed.

SEXUALITY

During REM sleep, men often have erections, and women's vaginas become more moist. This is perhaps explained by the fact that a common area of the brain influences both dreaming and sexual arousal. Sensual dream activity may leave the dreamer highly aroused on waking or may bring about a sexual climax.

Erotic dreams

Erotic dreams serve many purposes: they can be wish fulfilments or release of sexual frustration; they can provide exciting sexual encounters that are unavailable in the dreamer's waking life. If your dream lover gives you something that is not normally available to you, you may need to reassess your waking behavior. It may be that you need a little more excitement to enliven a dull relationship.

Homosexual dreams

If you are heterosexual, you may find it disturbing to dream of making love with a member of the same sex; but remember, you create your own dreams, so try to figure out what such a dream means to you. Perhaps it may enable you to empathize more closely with homosexuals; maybe it is trying to help you acknowledge an attraction that you do not acknowledge in your waking hours. There could be a more experimental side to your nature that you suppress for the sake of conformity.

Sex and guilt

Sometimes in sexual dreams you may find yourself engaged in activities that you would never think of in your waking life. Dreamers may be shocked and ashamed to discover they are having sex with a member of their family, or with a neighbor, or indulging in perverse or sado-masochistic sex—things they would never do in waking life. Dreams do not adhere to a moral code, and they come without censorship.

Sex is often associated with guilt and embarrassment, as in Ita's case:

I'm in bed with an unidenti-fied man. An old brass bed in a room with a window with a path outside; the drapes aren't drawn. A river is somewhere near. Having sex is pleasurable. The door opens and my mother walks in. I think, "Oh my God, I'll get found out."

If, as an adult, you experience anxiety about being found out, you need to give yourself permission to enjoy yourself or else discover what else you are doing that might make you feel guilty.

Creativity and sex

There is a strong link between sexual dreams and creativity, as Patricia Garfield reports in her book *Creative Dreaming*. Garfield concludes that freedom of activity in dreams is linked to the freedom of creative thinking in all areas.

Research has shown that creative people often have the most creative dreams, implying a strong relationship between the waking and sleeping mind.

JAMES'S DREAM
(16 YEARS OLD)

I dreamed that I went to the beach with my friend and on the beach was a naked girl. She looked foreign. My friend just disappeared and all of a sudden I was back home in bed with the foreign girl.

Our sexual dreams change with our age and experience. James's dream has much in common with those of others in his peer group. Not yet sexually active, James views a sexual encounter as mysterious, and a departure from his usual experience.

SUN

The sun, that life-giving source of light and energy, symbolizes masculinity, illumination, and consciousness in many cultures. In dreams, the sun's position in the sky—whether ascending or descending, whether it is rising in front of you or setting behind you—will give you information about a situation. The sun, which has been linked to the sun god Apollo, gives spiritual strength too, as Tania's dream shows:

TANIA'S DREAM

I am standing on a large rock in a desert. Small stones are scattered around. The sun is high in the sky. I am wearing a ram's head and robes bedecked with pentangles. I hold a staff in one hand and have a huge diamond ring on a finger on the other.

Slowly I raise my hand to the sun, which is very hot. The rays come down and split the diamond into all colors of the rainbow. They pass through the diamond in the ring and into my eye. As they do so, a great feeling of power enters me.

The sun, blazing out across a rocky landscape. The sun can signify consciousness, illumination, and masculinity.

Dreams about losing teeth do not necessarily reflect worries about dental health. They may symbolize broken relationships or times of change.

TEETH

Teeth are important dream symbols. As primitive personal weapons, they are linked to self-defense and attack. In many early societies, people wore the teeth of animals in necklaces or belts, as a sign of power and strength.

Teeth also represent the way we appear to the outside world. Teeth are so important to the image we present to the world at large that distressing teeth dreams often occur at times of change. These dreams may involve teeth crumbling, falling out, being blackened and decayed, or generally rotting in some way. However, as always, explore the simplest message of your dream first: do you need a dental check-up? Have you had a toothache or noticed a small cavity? If you are sure there is no physical trigger for your dream, consider other meanings.

Teeth-crumbling dreams may indicate a fear of getting older, of "falling apart" because of a personal crisis, of being less attractive to a partner at a time of relationship difficulties. They may indicate a parting from something or someone you have always been attached to, maybe even taken for granted.

Inez and her sisters all have excellent teeth so these dreams do not reflect waking worries about their dental health. After some discussion, we found that the dreams had come at a time of change within the family. Inez and her twin sister were at the point of going away to college for the first time. For each of them, their attachment was being broken and the loss of teeth symbolized this process of being separated.

Toothlessness

To dream of yourself as toothless, or to dream of an animal that has no teeth, often symbolizes a loss of power. The "bite" has gone, which means you cannot protect yourself as well as in the past and cannot "chew" on or tackle things as you have previously. Also, you cannot show your "fangs," your defensive barrier, to frighten off would-be assailants or negative people.

INEZ'S DREAM

My mother, sister, and I have all had the same very vivid dream, and each of us has had it more than once. This seems weird in itself, especially since it came to light after we had them, so we could not have inspired each other. It is simple really, we are just losing all our teeth or fillings and spitting them out by the hundred.

Dreams about war may be triggered by real experience, or may symbolize inner conflict.

WAR

Military conflict is represented in dreams in many ways, from guerrilla skirmishes to full-blown nuclear explosions. At a psychological level, war suggests turmoil, inner conflict, and internal struggles, perhaps between physical and spiritual desires.

Imagery of war is much more apparent in dreams at a time of military engagement such as during the Vietnam War or the Balkan crisis. They can occur to those people without personal experience of war. Angela had frightening dreams as a child during World War II:

> *I used to have a nightmare in childhood of Nazis coming down our lane. I would frantically try to secure the house, then barricade myself under the stairs. I found out later that my sister had this dream too.*

A contemporary nightmare—a nuclear war.

Nuclear war

The fear of total annihilation is expressed in dreams of nuclear explosions. The ultimate capacity for total destruction reveals, on one level, the realistic appreciation of the power of nuclear energy and, at another level, the destructive shadow side of ourselves and the power we hold to harm others.

> *I'm in a house with a friend. We are listening to the radio when a warning comes that a bomb is to be dropped. We lie down on the floor and cover our eyes with our hands. There is a blinding white light, which lasts a long time, as does the powerful heat. We try to leave the city but my legs are getting weaker, they are sore and hot. I wonder if I have sunburn or radiation sickness.*
>
> MARK

In dreams we may allow ourselves to explore the full implications of war, aspects that we tend to shy away from when awake. Experiencing this dream of total destruction made Mark determined to support antinuclear campaigns.

War language

Try interpreting your dream through language. When war appears in your dreams, see how it relates to your life. Has anyone dropped a bombshell on you? Do you feel as though you inhabit a war zone where conflict, sniping, and enemy fire are the order of the day? Even worse or more alarming might be the friendly fire aimed at you. What kind of war are you involved in? A war of words or a war of nerves? Are you on the warpath yourself or involved in a war of independence? Play around with the language of your dream whenever images of this type appear.

A dream battlefield may symbolize an antagonistic situation you face in your working life.

Crusades

Though war is usually shown as negative and destructive, it can also be seen as a crusade, a cleansing, a movement for change in a positive way. If you are on a crusade in your dream, what is it you passionately want to change?

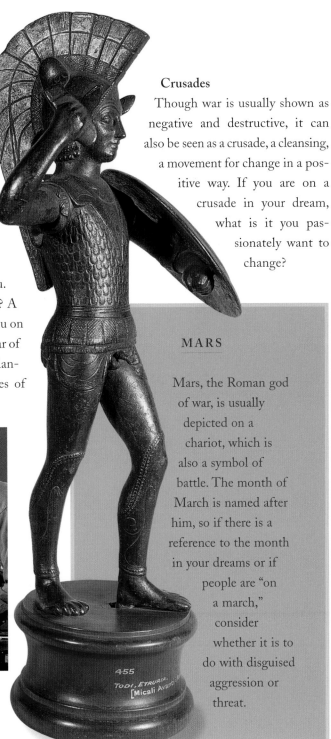

MARS

Mars, the Roman god of war, is usually depicted on a chariot, which is also a symbol of battle. The month of March is named after him, so if there is a reference to the month in your dreams or if people are "on a march," consider whether it is to do with disguised aggression or threat.

Being immersed in water in a dream reminds us of the security and warmth of the womb. This is a very positive, relaxing dream.

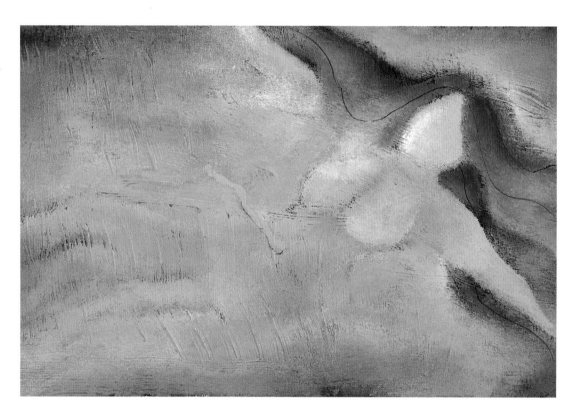

WATER

All life originated in water. The ancient Vedic texts refer to water as *matritamah*, "the most maternal." In dreams, the ocean symbolizes the mother, from which we all come. Water is associated with the unconscious, intuitive wisdom, and universal potential for creation. In some dreams, such as the one Zoe had, the symbolism of water as the life-giving force is very explicit:

> *There is a pool of water and I am attached to it by a cord connected to my stomach. Replenishment flows along the cord from the pool into me. This seems to be a womb dream.*

Bathing

If you are bathing or washing yourself in a dream it may represent an unconscious need for some form of cleansing. Do you feel that you need to make changes in your life? This could refer to career plans, your home, or a personal relationship. Think about what water and cleansing mean to you. Could they have spiritual or religious connotations, perhaps akin to baptism?

Swimming in a river or standing under a waterfall carries the same symbolism of immersion and purification. Think about what these activities mean to you, and how they may relate to the different areas of your life.

The transcendent nature of water

You cannot step twice in the same river; for fresh waters are ever flowing in upon you.

HERACLITUS (C. 500 BCE)

Water comes in many forms—clouds, ice, steam, flowing streams, or raging seas—making it a potent symbol of our complex emotional life, forever changing, in constant flux. The form that water takes in your dreams can give you a valuable message. Water in a canal, for example, is contained within artificial boundaries and flows in a defined path; it may represent the constraints in your life. In contrast, the unregulated power of water in the ocean carries a different message. Think also about the location of the water, and how you feel about being in that place.

Lara's dream of a menacing sea provided great insight into her situation:

I had a series of dreams of being menaced by the sea. I was very depressed at the time and the dreams became a focal point. I feel they saved my life.

Lara listened to the message in her dream and realized that she was being emotionally overwhelmed by circumstances in her life. When she began to acknowledge what was swamping her, her dreams moved from threat of drowning in rough seas to swimming in water that supported her.

Feeling happy and positive while in water indicates the dreamer is content and in control of his or her emotional life.

Whenever water appears in your dreams, examine the form the water takes in order to understand its message. Here are some questions to ask yourself:

- *Is the water clear or muddy?*

- *Are you swimming against the tide?*

- *Is the force of the waves overwhelming to you?*

- *Is the water calm and embracing?*

- *Are you naked or weighed down by inappropriate clothing?*

- *Do you feel confident in the water or out of your depth?*

4 | PSYCHIC DREAMS

Psychic, or psi, dreams take you one step farther into the mysterious realm of dreams. Many cultures believe that dreams are places where we can connect with our ancestors; other traditions talk of spirit guides appearing in dreams as guardian figures to steer individuals through difficult or traumatic times. Some forms of psychic dream can also take the dreamer into another dimension, such as dreams of astral travel.

Telepathic dreams or dreams of past lives and future events also feature in the range of psychic dreams. Whatever kind of psychic dream you may experience, keep an open mind—the power of the subconscious mind is not to be underestimated.

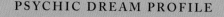

☽ | 4: Psychic dreams

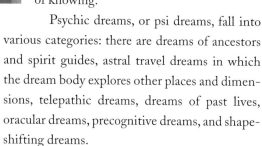

And it shall come to pass afterward that I shall pour out my spirit on all flesh; your sons and your daughters shall prophesy, your old men shall dream dreams, and your young men shall see visions.

JOEL 2:28

In antiquity there was no nation and practically no individual that did not believe in divine revelation through dreams. Whether those gods are still active today, or whether other explanations can be given for psychic dreams, they are still very much in evidence.

Edgar Cayce, who was born in 1877, was known as "the sleeping prophet," and was described as the father of psychic dreams. A gifted medical diagnostician and visionary, Cayce believed there are universal forces that we can contact according to our need and training. When we access these forces in dreams in the form of a "higher realm of the superconscious," we can be given information that we have no rational way of knowing.

Edgar Cayce was the first to identify the occurrence of psychic (or psi) dreaming.

Psychic dreams, or psi dreams, fall into various categories: there are dreams of ancestors and spirit guides, astral travel dreams in which the dream body explores other places and dimensions, telepathic dreams, dreams of past lives, oracular dreams, precognitive dreams, and shape-shifting dreams.

Psi dreams share certain characteristics; the box featured above contains a list of attributes that are common to psychic dreams.

PSYCHIC DREAM PROFILE

- *It feels very realistic, like a felt experience rather than a dream.*

- *The quality of light or color is different from your usual dreams.*

- *There is an unusually intense clarity.*

- *You have a sense of being warned or prepared.*

If a dream has these characteristics, make a note of it. By keeping a record of your dreams you can discover patterns in your dreaming and perhaps discover if you are having psychic dreams. Over a period of time, your dream journal will verify the accuracy of your psi dream predictions. Also, check with your family to see if anyone else has had the same or similar dreams because this ability often runs in families.

Cayce's research showed that some sensitive individuals can tune into psi communication. Like highly powered radio receivers, they pick up signals and information denied to less sensitive receivers. For some people, psychic phenomena happen more readily in dreams—the altered states of consciousness that occur nightly—because the vigilant waking censor in the mind does not immediately block them out.

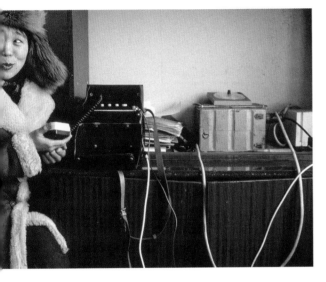

Consequently, these people are more open to the possibility of different forms of communication.

If you can accept that you are able to tune into another layer of communication, either because it is an inherited characteristic or because it has not been educated out of you, you will experience the gift of psychic dreams.

CONNECTING WITH OUR ANCESTORS

The unconscious is the reservoir of inherited ancestral and collective factors.

RAYMOND DE BECKER, *THE ANALYSIS OF DREAMS*

The earth where the dead are buried is the home of our ancestors. Connection with the earth offers the opportunity to reconnect and to communicate with those who have gone before us.

When people dream of caves, they evoke this ancestral connection. Cave dreams take us to the depths of mother earth and offer communication with the subterranean world that gives expression to our ancestral voices. The Sumerian word *matu* meant the sacred cave, the underworld, and the womb; this is also the universal root word for "mother." Our ancestors found shelter in caves, both from the elements and from predators, so not only were these important for survival but they often led deep into the heart of the earth.

Some people are like highly powered radio receivers and can use their sensitivity to "tune into" psychic signals in waking life and in dreams.

If you dream about a cave, or being inside a cave, you are making a connection with the earth and our ancestors.

A spirit guide may appear to a dreamer during a time of transition to give reassurance. They can take the form of a close friend or family member who has died.

SPIRIT GUIDES

During the dream state, inner wisdom may offer us glimpses into realms of which we may be completely unaware while we are awake. One example of this, which I have met again and again in my dream work with clients, is the appearance of a guide at transition points in life, particularly when the death of someone close is imminent. The guide, who is often a family member who has already died, comes back in the dream as an escort. This is what happened in Bill's dream:

Although my father was very ill, I never really thought about him dying from his illness until the day before his death. I dreamed I saw my late grandmother leading him away.

When we are visited in dreams by those who have died, they usually appear to give information or to give reassurance that they are with the dreamer in spirit though not in body. This feeling of being supported and cared for can be very reassuring, as Tricia relates:

It seems that the dreams I remember are very significant, as if someone, often relatives who have passed on, is emphasizing I am being looked after. I remember them for years after. They are imprinted on my memory.

The anima/animus (see page 26) can also be a helpful guide, showing you what you need in order to become more integrated and to help you have better relationships with partners.

Angels and devils

An angel appeared to Joseph and said "Joseph, thou son of David, fear not to take unto thee Mary, thy wife, for that which is conceived in her is of the Holy Ghost.

MATTHEW 1:20

The word "angel" is derived from a Greek word meaning messenger. In some religious traditions, angels are both guardians and escorts to heaven after death. They can give us aid on our path of spiritual development because they signify spiritual dimensions. In some societies, such as those of the Native North Americans, angels are known as spirits or spirit guides. These spirit messengers or angels are the mediators from God to human beings and come to help, particularly at times of extreme need.

Angels connect us to mystical experiences. "When you're dreaming, you're silent, and I think angels are attracted and allured by that," says Matthew Fox, an Episcopalian priest, in *The Physics of Angels*.

The angel represents your conscience, the "Jiminy Cricket" who knows what is the "right" thing to do. The devil, on the other hand, tempts you to bad behavior, the unwise course of action that your inner wisdom knows is bad for you. Angels and devils, symbols of good and evil, relate to the conflicting instincts of the dreamer.

Here the angel Gabriel is appearing to Joseph with a message from God. The word "angel" is derived from a Greek word for messenger, and the appearance of an angel in a dream heralds an important message.

We each have this duality, which at times can be very confusing and contradictory but which is basic human nature.

Finding a spiritual leader

Dreams of a spiritual leader often come at a point of crisis to give guidance or to help the dreamer find a path. They often have a powerful message. For some dreamers, the first intimation that there is about to be a spiritual dimension in their life comes in a dream.

When Tom was 18 years old, he dreamed of a man in white robes who told him that the beautiful cosmos that "danced" in front of him could be his. When he woke he was sad not to be in the wonderful world he had glimpsed, because he did feel that he had seen paradise. It was not until three years later that he came across a book in which there was a picture of the white-robed man who was a religious leader. Since then Tom's life has been devoted to the spiritual path of the guru he first met in his dream.

The appearance of a spiritual authority figure may foretell a new spiritual life for the dreamer.

SAM'S DREAM

*Twice I had an out-of-body experience.
I dreamed that I floated out of my body
around my bedroom and I could see
myself asleep and dreaming, looking
very snug and comfortable. This was a
weird experience but very nice and gave
a great feeling of satisfaction.*

*An out-of-body
experience is
often reported when
people are in life-
threatening
situations.
This can also
happen in dreams.*

ASTRAL TRAVEL

Unlike flying dreams, astral projection dreams are ones in which the dreamer feels he or she leaves the physical body and journeys to other places. These are sometimes called out-of-body experiences. Carol, a long-time student of psychic phenomena, has been aware of astral travel since childhood:

*I think it is important to understand about
astral travel. The spiritual body, the "subtle"
body, starts to detach itself from the feet
upward. Some people say this is changing
blood pressure. In one such dream I took a trip*

out of my body. I had my arms outstretched and was looking below me. It was very exhilarating, flying over trees, hills, and hedges. It made me feel I had escaped my prison and I was free. I felt much better.

I did feel fear when I realized that I had left my body, but maybe it was a healthy fear because you do have to take care in the astral plane and not get waylaid by lower entities.

The ancient Egyptians believed that part of the mind could separate itself from the rest; it was known as the *ka*. In Tibet, it is believed that we each have a spiritual replica, a twin, that holds our consciousness. The *bardo body*, as the twin is known, leaves the physical body at death but it can also leave the body temporarily in dreams and in meditative states of altered consciousness.

In *The Power of the Pendulum*, a study of precognitive dreams, the author T. C. Lethbridge confirms the view that the spirit, our astral body, travels as we sleep. The empty physical shell of the body remains in its sleeping position, but the astral body may go to the past, the future, or to other places existing in the present time.

Many ancient cultures believed that our consciousness, or "astral body," takes flight during sleep, enabling us to escape our regular experiences.

Flying dreams

There are many dreamers who have flying dreams before they go on to experience astral travel. In such dreams of being weightless, soaring over tops of buildings, hovering over the sea, or exploring other universes, the dreamer often has an exhilarating sense of adventure. Some people believe that these flying dreams are connections with impressions stored in our cells that reach back to our earliest ancestors who swam or flew at the very dawn of creation.

Flying dreams often precede astral travel.

Dreams can be a vehicle of telepathic communication from people who have died. Telepathy is especially strong between family members.

STEPHANIE'S DREAM

I dreamed that my husband sat up in the intensive care unit and indicated that he had had enough—he no longer wanted to live. I was wakened from this dream by the phone. It was the hospital to tell me that my husband was dying. Ten minutes later they phoned to tell me he was dead.

TELEPATHIC DREAMS

Telepathy is communication between two minds by some means other than the normal sensory channels. It appears that telepathy occurs most frequently with a member of our own family or with someone to whom we feel especially close.

Dreams can provide a way of communicating telepathically with people, especially loved ones, who have died. It is probable that some of these telepathic dreams reflect the important position certain people hold for us, and their views and the strong impression they leave can be revealed in dreams. Their presence engenders a feeling of being cared for, which in turn gives hope and reassurance.

Dreams can have psychic content in which figures, often family members, may predict forthcoming events.

GRACE'S DREAM

I dreamed I was in charge of a small hotel and was busy preparing for guests. I had a friendly German shepherd dog keeping me company. Everything was bright and clean but I felt worried because I needed some help to bring a barrel up from the cellar. There was a loud knock on the back door, and when I opened it, my mother's youngest brother and his youngest daughter Amy were there. In real life I had not seen this uncle for 20 years or more, or my cousin either. My uncle told me sadly that they had come to see me because they were going away. When I asked how long for, he said he wouldn't be back and they faded out of the picture.

I went on with my work and the dog lay on the mat watching me. There was another knock on the door and standing on the doorstep were my late mother and father. I welcomed them and asked if they had come to help me. They said very gently, "No, dear, we can't stay, we have a job to do." At that moment I awoke.

Grace felt sure she would have some family news, which she did:

At 10:30 my mother's sister phoned to say the uncle in my dream had passed away at 6 a.m. that day, and his youngest daughter Amy was with him at the time. At 1 p.m. that same aunt phoned again to tell me that my mother's oldest brother had also died that day. I could scarcely believe my ears. My parents had been gone for four years, my mother had always been close to her brothers and sisters.

*A mandala,
signifying eternal
life and
reincarnation.
Dreams about past
lives support the
Hindu and Buddhist
beliefs in
reincarnation.*

DREAMS OF PAST LIVES

Reincarnation is the belief that after we die we return to earth in another body, in a continuing cycle of death and rebirth. According to Hindu and Buddhist teachings, only when we have reached a state of enlightenment can we escape from the wheel of reincarnation and reach *nirvana*, the final release.

Edgar Cayce (see page 76) insisted that dreams may recall actual scenes, people, and memories from past lives. These often give clues about what it is the dreamer needs to work on in this incarnation, in order to improve both in spiritual and daily life. Cayce claimed that the purpose of dreaming of past lives was to enable the dreamer to hasten the development of his spiritual core.

Clare had a dream that felt so authentic that she was convinced she had actually met the man in the dream in a previous existence:

CLARE'S DREAM

I dreamed I was walking down a lane somewhere in France, Brittany perhaps. Coming toward me was a young soldier dressed in a French army uniform. Somehow he managed to explain the terrible futility of war. Even though I couldn't speak French, I understood and felt I'd known him all my life.

Jenny Cockell's book *Yesterday's Children* documents her search for the family she had been part of in a previous incarnation. She had experienced recurring dreams of being a woman named Mary, who had died feeling extreme guilt and anxiety about the young children she had left behind in the care of a violent and unreliable father. Jenny's dreams were so powerful that she was certain of the children's existence and eventually did reconnect with the family.

Dreams of past lives may show that death is not the end, merely the exchange of one place for another, one bodily form for another. Only you can determine whether your dream was reliving the memory of a past life or whether it was reflecting historical knowledge, or perhaps your subconscious knowledge of the future. Whatever your conclusions, the dream is still a message to yourself, and by interpreting it you gain more insight into yourself, physically, emotionally, and spiritually.

Dreamers may recall actual scenes and landscapes from past lives that are so vivid that they can be traced in their present lives.

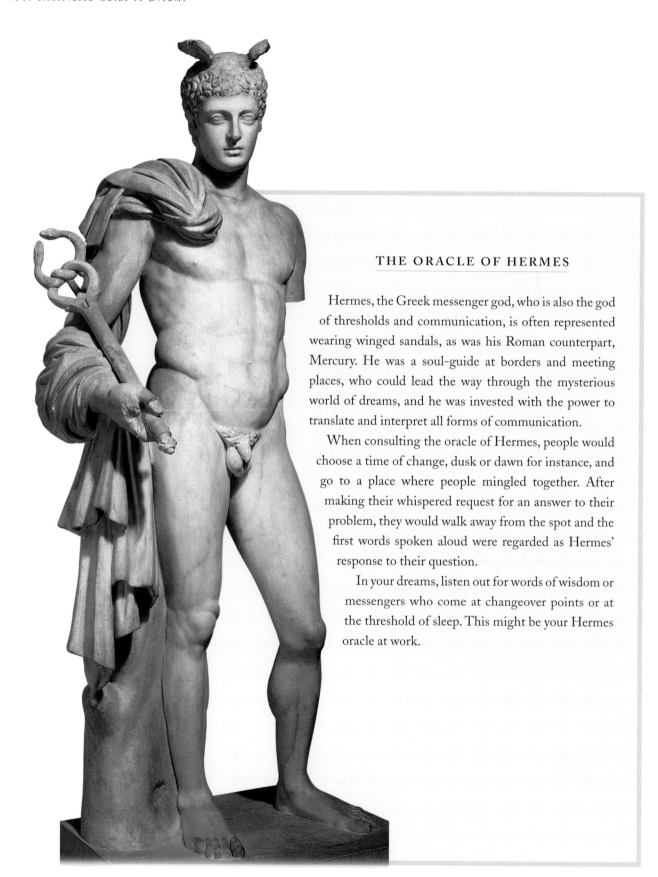

THE ORACLE OF HERMES

Hermes, the Greek messenger god, who is also the god of thresholds and communication, is often represented wearing winged sandals, as was his Roman counterpart, Mercury. He was a soul-guide at borders and meeting places, who could lead the way through the mysterious world of dreams, and he was invested with the power to translate and interpret all forms of communication.

When consulting the oracle of Hermes, people would choose a time of change, dusk or dawn for instance, and go to a place where people mingled together. After making their whispered request for an answer to their problem, they would walk away from the spot and the first words spoken aloud were regarded as Hermes' response to their question.

In your dreams, listen out for words of wisdom or messengers who come at changeover points or at the threshold of sleep. This might be your Hermes oracle at work.

Queen of Coins

Two of Cups

King of Coins

An oracle is an agency through which a prophecy is transmitted. It can be a sacred place or shrine, or an object such as the Tarot cards.

ORACULAR DREAMS

An oracle is a sacred place or shrine where deities are consulted for advice and prophecies. An oracle can also be a person or a thing. The I Ching and Tarot cards are used as oracles. In the majority of primitive cultures, the dream world was seen as the place where gods gave advice and directions about the future of individuals as well as that of the community. Such oracular dreams have led to the building of temples, the founding of cities, and the transformation of life.

Traditionally, dream diviners or interpreters have been temple priests, lamas, and shamans. Today, it is still widely held that dreams can be oracular; that is, they can indicate future events, whether or not they are requested. Modern dream diviners might be dream therapists or psychotherapists who help to illuminate the symbolic messages of dreams.

Oracular dreams sometimes feature Jungian archetypes. According to Carl Jung (see page 25), the function of these dreams is to weave into our lives our archaic heritage, allowing us to face the age-old threats and hopes that have been with us since the dawn of time.

Caves of oracles

Revelations were often spoken in caves such as the Delphic Oracle and in the grotto at Lourdes where the Virgin Mary appeared to St. Bernadette in 1858. Therefore, an oracular meaning is associated with caves in dreams; caves connect the upper and lower worlds, the light and the dark, the seen and the hidden. Caves are also associated with our ancestral origins and can signify that the dreamer is closely connected to the earth. A message received from, or in, a cave is therefore especially meaningful.

PRECOGNITIVE DREAMS

In precognitive dreams we dream of events before they occur in the waking world. Somehow, precognitive dreams tell of events that will happen in the future. They reveal a parallel reality, another dimension set in the future that is not always apparent in the noisy, busy world so many of us inhabit.

Precognitive dreams range from very explicit dreams to more symbolic ones. Trudi's precognitive dream was highly symbolic:

Two weeks before my grandmother died I dreamed I was walking with her on a frozen beach. We saw a huge wave which froze at its highest point and cracked. She fell down by my side.

Stella's precognitive dream shows how dreams can transmit psychic information that we may have picked up on a subconscious level:

I was walking along the beach at Formby Point (near Southport, England) where I often walk my dog. The sea was very rough and a man in the sea was calling to me for help. Although I tried to get to him my legs were very heavy and I could only watch him sink.

Dreaming about an event that later takes place cannot be rationally explained, but we do know that this has been happening for centuries.

When she woke up Stella told her husband about the dream. At her usual time, 7:15 a.m., she drove to work. A report came on the radio about a man's body being found on the beach at Formby Point. "I felt quite ill for a couple of weeks afterward," she said. "And neither I nor my husband could explain why I should have such a dream." Stella did not know the man.

Was it a coincidence? An ultrasensitivity to another person's distress? Perhaps a resonance with a place? While there is no "rational" explanation, Stella can take comfort from the fact that throughout history and still today, thousands of other people have had equally inexplicable experiences of psychic information.

There are many examples throughout history of precognitive dreams: Calpurnia, Caesar's wife, dreamed of his assassination; Abraham Lincoln foresaw his own death in a dream; Oliver Cromwell dreamed he was to become the greatest man in England; the British boxer Sugar Ray Robinson dreamed that his punch would kill opponent James Doyle.

Precognitive dreams can be extremely valuable, particularly when they warn the dreamer of an event that he or she can then take steps to avert, or when the dream prepares the dreamer in such a way that it eases any subsequent distress. As Carol told me:

When there is a warning element it is important not to ignore it because, although certain events cannot be prevented, they can be made less serious in their consequences. Other times accidents and mishaps can be prevented, so it is good to get over the feelings of alarm and do what common sense tells you and so avoid "if only I had acted on it" feelings.

English general and politician Oliver Cromwell (1599–1658) experienced a precognitive dream about his rise to power.

OLIVERIVS CROMWEL
ANGLICÆ REIP. PRO- TECTOR. EIVSDEMQ,
EXERCITVM DVX GENERALIS, ETC.

GINA'S DREAM

I have had disturbing dreams before a disastrous personal event, like that of my brother's death, where I dreamed of a funeral in a church where even the altar cloth was black and there were waves beating against the stained-glass windows. I come from a family of spiritualists, though I am not one myself, and most of my relatives have experienced death premonitions. I believe my own dreams reflect my subconscious awareness that something seems set to happen.

reveals the common conflict a child sometimes feels about a parent, when love gives way to fear as the child sees another side of the parent.

I am upstairs in my bedroom, aged about six or seven, and suddenly the house is full of dwarfs. I rush downstairs to tell my mother and when I do, I realize she is in league with them and she becomes one.

A person who has been sexually abused may dream of a lover's face changing into the face of the past abuser. Where this happens, professional counseling may be needed to deal with the unfinished trauma.

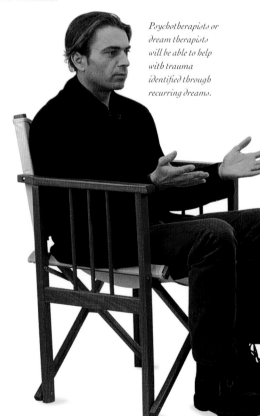

Psychotherapists or dream therapists will be able to help with trauma identified through recurring dreams.

SHAPE-SHIFTING DREAMS

In dreams often anything is possible. For example, you can be transformed from one person into another, or from an animal into a human being, or from a living creature into an inanimate object. This phenomenon is known as shape-shifting and can signify change or ambiguity. In Polly's dream her dogs change form:

If you dream about something changing shape, compare the meaning of the object or person before, during, and after the change.

I was standing in a garden with our white Chihuahua dogs when out of the door of a house came a minister and his wife and he spoke to me. Suddenly, the dogs turned into white doves and flew into the air.

The shape-shifting of her dogs into doves of peace meant the end of a period of stress for Polly.

If you have an ambivalent relationship with another person, a love-hate tug, your dreams may show the person changing form. Anika's dream

Centaur: part man, part horse, a centaur symbolizes the untamed, instinctive side of humankind.

Garuda: half man and half eagle, it is a powerful symbol of retribution and a destroyer of evil.

Sphinx: four creatures combine to make a sphinx, symbolizing the four natural elements of earth, wind, fire, and water.

Harpy: part woman, part bird, a harpy is associated with storms and sudden death.

Hybrids

In dreams we meet people or creatures that are a combination or mixture of different people, elements, or animals. These often represent symbolic attributes, and thus, since all creation is interconnected in the web of life, they show how contrasting aspects of the dreamer come together. Think about what the individual components of the creature or person may be telling you, and also about how you feel toward it. Here is a list of the most common hybrids:

• Centaur, part man, part horse, symbolizes the instinctual, untamed side of humankind.

• Chiron, the most gentle of centaurs who is often depicted as wounded, symbolizes nature's healing power.

• Garuda, half man and half eagle, is the destroyer of evil-doers, the enemy of snakes, and a symbol of retribution.

• Sphinx, with the head of a human, body of a bull, feet of a lion, and wings of an eagle, combines four creatures to symbolize the four elements. This creature represents wisdom and the riddle of existence.

• Harpy, with the body of a woman and the wings and legs of a bird, is a wind spirit who can summon winds and cause storms; it is said to be responsible for sudden deaths.

Incubus and succubus

In early Christianity these creatures were considered to be the devil in a transformed state. Because sex was usually associated with the devil's work, it was believed that the incubus, the male form, and the succubus, the female form, visited sleeping men or women to make love to them. Dreaming about a devil-like figure can indicate that something is worrying the dreamer.

5 | DREAMS AND CREATIVITY

For centuries writers, artists, and performers have all been inspired by their dreams to push the creative boundaries of their art. Surrealists such as Salvador Dali used dreams to create astonishing works of art. Some of the greatest stories ever told began life as dreams. Without the inspiration of a dream great inventions may never have seen the light of day—who would have guessed that the formulation of the quantum theory was completed with the help of a dream?

By learning to embrace wholeheartedly the rich imagery and symbolism in your dreams, however bizarre they may seem, you will be able to unlock your own creative potential.

5: Dreams and creativity

Dreams are part of our creative life. Imagination and creativity blossom in the unconscious mind to provide new insights, original ways to solve problems, and ideas that enrich our artistic nature.

ARTISTS AND DREAMS

Creativity and imagination can blossom in a dream state. Many famous artists have been inspired by images that appear in dreams.

Throughout history, people have been inspired by dreams to create works of art. Many painters have seen images in their dreams that subsequently translated onto canvas or into the written word. Arthur Rackham, a great British

illustrator and painter, used inspirational dreams as the basis for many of his paintings, as did William Blake, the poet and artist.

Surrealists such as Max Ernst, René Magritte, and Salvador Dali owed much to dream inspiration. They deliberately tried to recreate the dream state by juxtaposing unusual objects that rationally did not fit together, as in Magritte's painting *Golconde*, where bowler-hatted men drop from the sky instead of raindrops. Odilon Redon painted parts of his dreams and nightmares. Fantastic creatures emerge from the depths of his surrealistic evocations and threaten waking security.

Dreams have inspired many poets. The poem "Kubla Khan" was dreamed by Samuel Taylor Coleridge, and on waking he remembered distinctly about 300 lines. However, the ending escaped him when someone called to the house and delayed him for over an hour. By then he had forgotten the final 10 lines but recalled enough to complete them. Without the dream we might never have had this world-famous poem.

Graham Greene used dreams to help in his novel writing. Robert Louis Stevenson regularly dreamed of his "Brownies;" these dream visitors gave him stories, and generally directed his creative life. Stevenson's classic *Doctor Jekyll and Mr. Hyde* was also dream-inspired.

The novels of magic realists such as Gabriel Garcia Marquez and Isabel Allende have the dreamlike quality of strange characters performing bizarre feats where the unexpected and fantastical become the stuff of everyday life.

FIONA'S DREAM

Afraid of being harshly judged, Fiona, a talented poet, repressed her creative side and stopped writing. When this happened, anxiety dreams tormented her and culminated in a dream in which she was being chased by a female vampire through a series of dark, twisting tunnels.

When I woke up, I knew I had to get back to writing poetry because all those tunnels were about my trying different ways to please other people but they were leading nowhere. And the vampire was really a part of myself that wanted to suck out my life's blood, because I know now, that without expressing that creative part of me I might as well be a zombie, which is what happens to you after a vampire gets you.

Fiona was fortunate. She was able to recognize that her dream self was wise. She had used her dreams for creativity and well-being in the past and knew how to interpret them.

Repressing your creative thoughts can have a damaging psychological effect, and dreaming about being lost can be a warning sign.

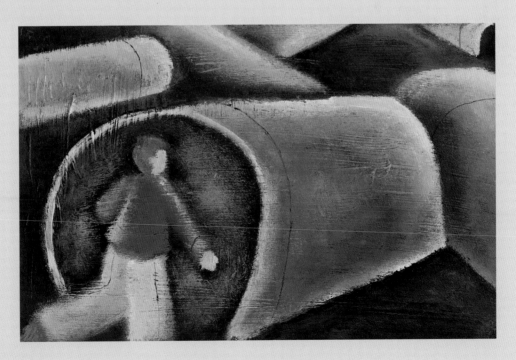

COLOR

Color is a vital part of both the writer's and painter's palette. In dreams, color has a particular importance, as it does in waking life. Not only are we affected by the energy vibrations of color, as I explain in detail in my book *Creative Visualization with Color*, but each color has mythical and symbolic associations. If a particular color is predominant in a dream, it may be sending you a message. This brief guide will help you appreciate the symbolic significance of color in your dreams:

I dream in Technicolor, with sound, smell, taste—everything. Some people have told me they dream in black and white, or silently. This has amazed me. My dreams are like being there.

DEAN

I dream in color, my husband says he only dreams in black and white.

MARINA

- Blue: devotion, religion, faithfulness, infinity of sea and sky

- Black: the underworld, the occult, earth, fecundity

- Red: strong emotion, anger, blood, earthy desires

- Green: fertility, the cycles of nature, balance, healing

- Gray: pallor, ashes, lack of energy, apathy, fatigue

- Pink: innocence, gentleness, love, vulnerability

- Purple: power, high rank, nobility, spiritual development

- Violet: memories, insight, devotion

- Yellow: energy, warmth, intelligence and intellectual development

- White: purity, clarity, unblemished innocence

INVENTIONS

Part of the process of dreaming involves scanning all our stored memories so that we can file new information and experiences into recognizable categories based on previous experiences and past events. For example, if one day you were almost hit by a car as you walked across the road, you might dream of a previous frightening experience you had in childhood or about another car that caused you problems in the past. Your dream will put together events from your current life with whatever events from your past are most useful for you to recall. Now, what has this to do with inventors?

Many inventors have brilliant flashes of inspiration or make world-changing scientific discoveries via their dreams; this is because the dream completes their waking work in their area of expertise. Here are some examples:

Danish physicist Niels Bohr (1885–1962) was awarded the Nobel prize for physics in 1922 for his formulation of the quantum theory. After grappling for months with the problem of how basic elements existed and how they maintained stability he could not figure out the solution. One night he dreamed that he was at the races. The horses ran in clearly marked lanes, which they could change if they maintained a precise distance from each other. When he woke he knew that the "rule of the track" applied to electrons as they orbited their atom. The dream solution completed his waking work and his findings revolutionized our understanding of the universe.

Albert Einstein (1879–1955) said that a dream he had as a young man inspired his

scientific research. In the dream he was sleighing down a mountainside at the speed of light. He noticed that the refracted light of the stars curved into a spectrum of colors, and he was so deeply moved by this that he puzzled over it and thought about it for days on end. He said that eventually it led him to the theory of relativity.

The German chemist F.A. Kekulé (1829–1896) dreamed of a snake swallowing its own tail; the symbolic meaning of this image made complete sense to him in terms of the problem he was working on in his waking life. It represented the structure of the benzene molecule. The dream was a cipher, a symbolic representation of the answer to his question.

Dimitri Mendeleyev (1834–1907), a Russian chemist, found the solution to the construction of the periodic table of elements in a dream. He fell asleep listening to chamber music and dreamed that the basic elements were linked to each other in the same way that melodies are.

Elias Howe (1819–67), US inventor of a sewing machine using two threads, dreamed of spears being thrown at him. At the tip of the spears were oval holes. At last he knew where to put the eye of the needle so that his invention would work.

In conclusion, the process of dreaming enables us to organize our waking thoughts. This could enable you to see things in a new way to solve problems or find inspiration.

The field of quantum physics owes much to a dream. Niels Bohr's dream about a horse race enabled him to complete his theory.

6 | DREAMS AND HEALTH

You can make dreams work for you by using them to help improve your mental or physical health. Ancient physicians analyzed dreams to find cures and today many practitioners who take a holistic approach to illness use dreams as a diagnostic tool. Your dream journal can help you recognize patterns in your dreams that reveal the body's hidden messages to the mind about your physical or psychological state.

The therapeutic value of dreams is also well known; dreams have helped many patients come to terms with illness or disability. People who have undergone traumatic events find that reliving them in dreams helps them to cope and ultimately find closure to a painful experience.

☾ | 6: Dreams and health

Some dreams are divinely inspired and others are the direct result of the physical body.

HIPPOCRATES (C.460–370 BCE)

Dreams play a crucial part in maintaining our positive physical and emotional health. Throughout history dreams have been used in the diagnosis and treatment of all types of illness — physical, mental, emotional, and spiritual. In many cases, these healing journeys include the abstract transcendent, that sense of God, the universe, or a higher spiritual force, which creates a mystical dimension that goes beyond our everyday experience.

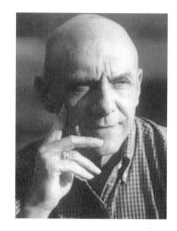

Dr. Bernie Siegel, American cancer surgeon and author, believes that dreams can help in the healing process.

Dreams can sometimes bring healing experiences that impart a sense of a higher spiritual force and create a mystical dimension that transcends our everyday lives.

USING DREAMS TO HEAL

Dream interpreters in ancient Greece were sought after in much the same way as doctors are today. Using dreams, they would diagnose and offer remedies for all manner of physical and emotional ills. The Greek physicians Hippocrates and Artemidorus, and their Roman successor Galen, all promoted the use of dreams in diagnosis and treatment and this is still practiced today.

American cancer surgeon and author Dr. Bernie Siegel uses dreams to help his patients identify ways in which they can most effectively combat their disease. His fascinating results described in *Love, Medicine, and Miracles* show how dreams give information that is not readily available to the waking mind. He also describes how dreams can reassure the patient.

Dreams have been used for the diagnosis and treatment of illness since the time of Hippocrates, in ancient Greece.

At a conference I attended, Dr. Siegel told how he dreamed he was at a meeting for a group of cancer sufferers. At the time he was undergoing investigative tests because of an undiagnosed condition. In the dream, one of the members turned to him and told him he should not be in the group because he did not have cancer. Siegel woke convinced that he no longer needed to fear a diagnosis of cancer, and he was proved right.

Dreams can also help in the healing process by bringing hope when all seems lost. After his accident, Tad's dreams were focused on his recovery:

> *Last November I had a terrible car accident. The doctors did not know if I would be able to walk again and thought for a while they would have to amputate my legs. Luckily they did not. I spend a lot of time in a wheelchair but I can walk a little. I tell you this because for a long time my dreams were almost the same: walking, legs, feet, shoes, etc. And as I am starting to have a normal life again, my dreams are changing, returning more to how they were before the accident.*

PRODOMIC DREAMS

Prodomic dreams signal the presence of an illness before it is outwardly manifest. The word "prodomic" comes from the ancient Greek *prodomos*, meaning "running before." Belief in the power of prodomic dreams, also known as diagnostic or endoscopic dreams, dates back to antiquity and is widespread today.

HIPPOCRATIC CORPUS

The Hippocratic Corpus, the body of work written by Hippocrates, the father of modern medicine, outlines the ways in which dreams deal with waking events or daytime residue. Hippocrates believed that dreams that contradict daytime activity indicate bodily disturbance. For example, if the sun, moon, and stars behave strangely, the dreamer should take heed: "When the heavenly bodies wander in different directions some mental disturbance as a result of anxiety is indicated."

Since antiquity, people have believed that dreams can offer guidance. Hippocrates believed that if a person dreamed about a heavenly disturbance it indicated anxiety in the dreamer.

Diagnostic dreams have been compared to lenses because they make the causes of ill-health more visible.

In the Middle Ages, Arnald of Villanova compared diagnostic dreams to lenses because they made the source of ill-health more visible to the physician. Medard Boss in his book *The Analysis of Dreams* (see page 124) cites the example of a patient Villanova treated. On two occasions the patient dreamed that his ear was being beaten by a stone. On examination there was nothing obviously wrong with the man's ear, but shortly afterward he developed a serious inflammation in the same ear that had been beaten in the dream.

If you dream that part of your body is injured or damaged, at an unconscious level you may know there is something wrong even though there may be, as yet, no obvious overt signs.

Dreams can signal illness and we should try to stay attuned to their messages to protect our health. So always check with a doctor if your dreams refer to personal ill-health.

Here are some examples of prodomic, or diagnostic, dreams:

For months Amy had been having dry eyes, a problem that had defeated several ophthalmic consultants. She dreamed that her eye condition was directly linked to breastfeeding her young baby. She was so certain the dream was accurate that she told her doctor about it. He at last made the connection between breastfeeding, dry eyes, and dehydration. The dream had revealed a previously overlooked cause, making the diagnosis quite clear.

Nerys Dee, in her book *Your Dreams and What They Mean* (see page 124), describes the case of a man who had recurrent fevers that his doctor could not diagnose. One night the man dreamed he passed a pharmacy window and saw a sign that said "tonic." When he woke he thought he would buy a tonic from the pharmacy, but on his journey he passed a store selling alcohol. In the window were several bottles of Indian tonic water, and he decided that this was the "tonic" in his dreams and he should try it. After drinking a number of bottles of the Indian tonic water his fever disappeared. An important ingredient in Indian tonic water is quinine. Quinine was, at one time, a standard treatment of malaria and other fevers, though consciously the man was not aware of this.

Your dreams may provide vital clues for self-diagnosis. One man dreamed that tonic water would cure his fevers, which proved to be correct.

This mother had a diagnostic dream that revealed a previously overlooked explanation.

DREAMING OF HEALERS

If you dream of a doctor, it may mean that you need to consult one or that you have an authoritative, healing aspect of yourself you can access. Clearly, as with all other figures in dreams, you need to make connections relevant to your life since your unique dream has special meaning to you. Is the figure someone you recognize, albeit in the guise of a doctor? Are they trying to tell or show you something—perhaps draw your attention to a part of your body?

Monks in a dream may symbolize healing. The association between monks and the healing arts can be traced back through the centuries because hospital care and refuge was first offered in monasteries.

The appearance of a monk in a dream may signify healing since hospital care was first offered in monasteries, as was refuge and protection.

Dreams of nurses also relate to healing. Look to your own self-healing capabilities: what can you do to help yourself feel better? Consider the implications of the language itself; the word nurse is used in phrases such as "to nurse a grudge" and "nurse a drink," which means to hold onto something, to make it last longer. Are you harboring any ill-will that you could let go of? Are you holding onto an emotion, a relationship, a habitual way of thinking or behaving which is no longer useful? If so, now is the time for reexamination to jettison the clutter out of your life.

DREAMS, DRUGS, AND ADDICTION

Drugs alter body chemistry, which in turn affects our dreams. Sleeping pills, antihistamines, and alcohol all affect REM sleep profoundly, as do antianxiety drugs such as tranquilizers and amphetamines. Some antidepressant drugs also inhibit or erase dreaming sleep.

I have had nightmares especially when I was coming off sleeping pills, which I was addicted to at the time.

EMMA

Although Lucy did not use drugs herself, her husband's addiction was influencing her life. She had this disturbing dream:

Alcohol and drugs can disrupt our sleep patterns, which over a long period of time can affect our mental well-being.

LUCY'S DREAM

I was going to visit someone. I had to go through parts of the high-rise apartments but the middle part was a mental hospital. Then I was being attacked by crocodiles. They cornered me.

Lucy's husband is a heroin addict and his erratic outbursts have all the characteristics of mental illness, which is why she dreamed of the image of her apartment building as a mental hospital. The crocodile, because of its destructive power and viciousness, symbolized evil and fury for the ancient Egyptians; because it inhabits a place between earth and water, it also represents a knowledge of and movement between the borderlands. The crocodile attack depicts Lucy's feelings of assault from the unpredictable and marginal world of drug-induced unreality, with all its destructive strength. Although Lucy knew nothing of these ancient connections, her dream was able to tap into the collective unconscious. The dream therefore vividly portrays her perilous state, which is endangering her both physically and mentally.

Frequent disruption of REM sleep can have a damaging effect on mental health. Dreaming is vital for our minds to make sense of thoughts and feelings.

Crocodiles and scorpions symbolize evil and viciousness for many cultures. Dreaming about dangerous animals may be a warning about personal danger.

Dream rebound

The dream rebound is what makes it so hard for people who are hooked on sleeping drugs to get off them. The first night there is usually highly disturbed sleep that is virtually all REM and full of anxiety dreams and nightmares. This can be a terrifying experience and can cause the dreamer to return to the drugs. Withdrawal from the chronic use of sleep medications must therefore always be done very gradually, preferably under the supervision of a doctor.

Self-help

If you have a problem with addiction, or fear that you might be addicted, to alcohol for example, use the dream incubation method on pages 118–119 to ask for guidance. You might incubate a question such as "How can I drink less given that all my business meetings involve alcohol?" or "Why do I need to drink to excess?" Your dream answers may give you reasons as well as solutions, though professional help is very important if the addiction is causing problems generally.

Dreaming about drinking alcohol may be your body warning you of a problem with alcohol addiction.

In addition to giving us information, I think dreams are actually physically necessary. I used to take a lot of speed, which meant little sleep and little dreaming, and when I stopped all I did was sleep for weeks and my dreams were particularly vivid. I felt I was catching up on my dreaming more than my sleeping; the dreams just did not stop from the moment I fell asleep to waking up. People I have checked this with have said they felt the same thing.

THERESA

Discussing your dreams with a professional therapist can be a vital part of a healing process.

DREAMS AND THERAPY

Dreams can have a vital role to play in psychotherapy because patients, by talking about their dreams to their therapists, can uncover the hidden aspects of themselves and their problems. As Nor Hall says in her book called *The Moon and the Virgin*, "Exchanging words is the essence of psychotherapy." When we talk about dreams, what is illuminated is the deep well of hurts and hindrances that blight our lives, as well as the power of our healing potential and inner wisdom.

In our dreams we wrestle with our problems, and in therapy we harness our dreams' energy and the subconscious to guide us toward greater self-awareness and well-being.

NAZ'S DREAM

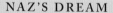

In one dream I was introduced to two people, both with the same name, who were different parts of the same person. In the dream I introduced them to each other. I woke up seeing the two as halves of the same person, saying: "Confront yourself with yourself, himself with himself."

This dream paved the way for the resolution of former fragmentation and brought a new feeling of wholeness in Naz's life.

DREAMS AND YOUR WELL-BEING

I am sure that in a sense dreams are pure chemistry, and that certain chemical balances and imbalances fire certain brain cells. My most intense dreaming periods have been after operations, one to remove the ovaries, the second to remove part of the thyroid, both traumatic glandular changes.

GAYLE

Illness is not purely the result of imbalances in body chemistry or the invasion of deadly organisms; there is also a psychological component to illness. How we feel about ourselves and our lives alters our capacity to deal with stress and our resistance to disease. When we sleep, our mind does not have to concern itself with external stimuli, so it can focus on the internal world of the body and psyche and reflect information about our psychological state and mental well-being back to us through our dreams. These dreams warn us of impending health problems and help us ward off illness.

By recording your dreams over a period of time you may discover themes that predict or reveal your physical or psychological state. For instance, people suffering from migraines who have made a note of dream patterns have learned which dream images come before a full-blown attack and are able to take preventive medication. Dr. Robert Smith, an American cardiologist, presented research at the Association for the Study of Dreams that showed that the efficiency of the pumping mechanism of the heart is directly related to particular dream images.

Similarly, certain dream images can precede nocturnal asthma attacks.

May recorded her dreams for a year or so and began to see a dream pattern that would occur just before she became ill:

If I'm going to become ill, a few days before, I dream that all the walls in my bedroom begin to close in on me. Even the ceiling gets lower and it is all really vivid.

To someone else the dream might symbolize something completely different—for example a claustrophobic sexual relationship or a feeling of being trapped perhaps—but in this case May understands the pattern of her dream signals, so she knows that this dream indicates that she is under par.

Our ability to deal with stress and illness is related to our sleep and dream patterns.

107

Catatonic, rigid figures have warned dreamers of ill-health, signifying that the body is not functioning correctly.

Before her depression was diagnosed, Naomi had a series of dreams that troubled her:

> *There is a small isolated cottage in a rural landscape that I do not recognize. It is a flat, desolate landscape, gray, and dark.*

Take note of the setting of your dreams. A cheerless, remote landscape may indicate depression.

The setting of this recurring dream is important. It depicts isolation, remoteness, and flatness, all of which are characteristics of depression. Add to that the gloom of gray and the lack of any brightness and we have an even clearer indication of a low mood. Bearing in mind that a house often represents the dreamer, it is significant that the small cottage is alone, far from any other person, and is vulnerable, which directly mirrors how life was for Naomi during this period. The fact that this dream theme persisted caused Naomi to pay attention to it. Before the dreams began, she had recognized her own symptoms of depression, which is the case for so many who suffer from this "malignant sadness," as Lewis Wolpert so eloquently expresses it in his book *The Malignant Sadness* (see page 124).

Dreams have played a part in the diagnosis of severe mental illness since earliest times. Sometimes they show the complete fragmentation of the self. Medard Boss, in his brilliant book *The Analysis of Dreams,* explains how psychosis, or complete mental breakdown, may be indicated in dreams many years before the event. Boss cited the case of a young woman who dreamed that she called her family to dinner. Her two sisters, who were sitting on a bed, turned to stone, then her mother and father turned to stone. She rushed up to her father, threw her arms around his neck but

he crumpled to sand. This dream recurred four times over a period of a week. Eventually a day came when she was taken ill with a severe form of schizophrenia, displaying catatonic features in which the body becomes rigid, like stone.

Such catastrophic dreams will not mean the same to each of us. However, if you respond to your dreams and value their potential to warn or prepare you for illness, you have a greater chance of taking preventive action and so maintaining good health.

TRAUMA AND DREAMS

One of the characteristics of post-traumatic stress disorder is recurrent nightmares. The nightmares, as well as waking flashbacks of the event, can continue to cause extreme distress. Past trauma can so easily threaten the present when it comes back in terrifying dreams.

Dreams can sometimes help the dreamer to recall memories of a trauma that the waking mind has blocked out. People who experience accidents, for example, and wake up in the hospital often have no recall of the events that hospitalized them. Billie's car was rammed by a truck, which pushed her into the path of an oncoming car. The injuries she suffered were severe and she was rushed from the scene of the accident to intensive care. Though she quickly regained consciousness, she did not know what had happened until she dreamed about being cut out of her car by fire officers. Her dreams gradually provided more and more information as she grew stronger and more able to bear the shock of the events. Dreams following trauma frequently provide sufficient information to complete the puzzle of the events that surrounded it.

Traumatic events such as experiencing severe fear, attack, rape, or war cause utter shock to the whole system, which results in nightmares. Susan's horrific dream echoed a traumatic childhood experience:

> I dreamed I was in a church. Naked corpses were piled up on the inner window ledges. I was locked in and couldn't get out no matter how hard I tried. I woke up screaming.

A real-life trauma can produce nightmares, causing additional stress and anxiety to the dreamer.

Susan's dream about being trapped in a church (see page 109) and unable to escape repeated a real life experience.

Susan used to sleep in her mother's bed when her father was working away from home. When she was seven she woke up to find her mother dead beside her. Alone in the house, in her terror she could hardly unlock the doors to get out and tell someone what had happened. The church image links to her experience of her mother's open coffin at the funeral, which intensified her trauma.

The recurrent nightmare that Ailsa experiences is short and simple, but no less terrifying for that: "I dream of a gray-haired man chasing me and getting hold of me." This is a repetition of an event that happened when she was 12 years old. Though she escaped before the man could inflict physical harm, the shock of the event is reenacted in dreams whenever she goes through a period of stress.

In these types of dreams your subconscious mind is trying to find a way of avoiding the shock, to find another solution to the traumatic experience. By addressing these fears when you are awake, you will find that the dreams become less intrusive and will change as you come to terms with your traumatic experience.

Dreams are a safe way to relive, and relieve, painful or threatening situations from past experience. The dreams release some of the psychological pressure and act as a safety valve so that the emotional tension does not become overwhelming. However, if you do have recurring nightmares, try the techniques given on page 118. If they still persist, seek professional help. You might find that the act of recording your dreams may help you cope with the trauma.

SHAMANS AND HEALERS

The word "shaman" came originally from Siberia and describes priests and healers who work with spirit helpers in the form of animals or birds. Shamans and healers can be found in many cultures, including those of certain Native North Americans, some African societies, and the Aborigines of Australia.

Shamanism is based on the belief in a world pervaded by good and evil spirits that can be controlled and influenced. Through altered states of consciousness, including dreaming, the shaman travels beyond death and time. Figures met in these dream journeys are considered every bit as real and important as those encountered in waking life, and they sometimes reveal future events that are in store for the community or individuals.

The shaman interprets images seen in dreams and uses them to cure illnesses. In healing rituals, the shaman or healer sometimes takes certain drugs, local psychedelic substances such as peyote, for instance, in order to "see" the roots of illness and know which cure to give.

Part of the power of shamanism depends on the union of the female and male aspects; the male priest often dresses in women's clothes to recreate symbolically the original, perfect state that existed before the sexes were separated. If you dream of wearing clothes of the opposite sex, explore the possibility that you need more of that gender's traditional qualities to bring you balance and wisdom.

Shamans have often been depicted dressed as stags because these animals are associated with both wisdom and virility. Also, the shaman mask was sometimes made in the zigzag shape of a lightning flash, which symbolizes the ability to move between the earthly and heavenly worlds. To be struck by lightning, in the shamanic tradition, was a sign of initiation, so if you dream of lightning you may be being inspired toward new spiritual developments.

Shamans (healers or medicine men) are common to many cultures, including Native Americans, African societies, and Australian Aborigines.

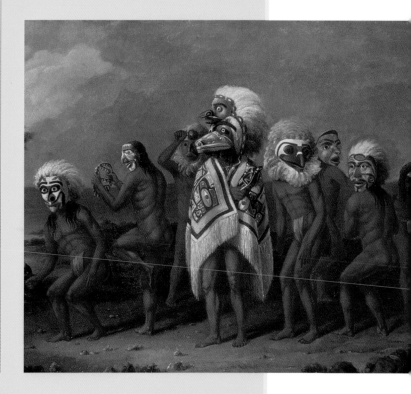

7 | ENRICHING YOUR DREAM LIFE

Using your dream life to full advantage will bring a wide range of benefits. By learning lucid dreaming techniques, you can replay negative events or situations in your dreams in order to effect a positive outcome. Visualization helps you to explore this dream concept while awake, by enabling you to program your mind to cope effectively with difficult situations. Solutions can also be found using dreams—by "sleeping on it" the subconscious mind will show you how to approach a tricky problem from a different perspective.

You should now be fully aware of the importance of dreams and the potential they have to empower your waking life. Sweet dreams!

7: Enriching your dream life

As you have seen in the preceding chapters, dreams can enrich your life in a whole variety of ways. They can inspire artistic creativity, help you solve problems, diagnose illness, and show you how to protect and improve your mental and physical well-being. Dreams can lead to a new understanding of personal problems in your waking life and improve relationships. They can also provide therapy to help cope with past traumatic experiences. Dreams can also connect us to other realms of existence, or to past cultures beyond the reach of the conscious, waking mind.

Lucid dreamers know they are dreaming, and can control the events and content of their dream.

LUCID DREAMING

For lucid dreamers there is the additional dimension of control. In lucid dreaming you know you are dreaming while you are still in the dream. The "lucid" part refers to the clarity of consciousness, your clear awareness, rather than the vividness of the dream. Lucid dreamers can deliberately employ the natural creative potential of dreams for problem solving and artistic inspiration. Athletes, entertainers, performers, or anyone who gives presentations can prepare, practice, and polish their performances while they sleep.

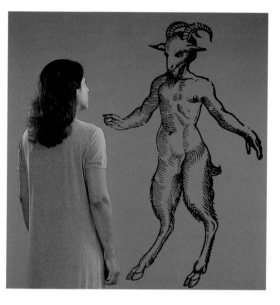

Some lucid dreamers can create a complete fantasy world, and experience anything they can imagine.

DAVID'S DREAM

In one of my lucid dreams I was shot in my arm, which immediately started pouring with blood and made me fall to the floor. I suddenly thought what is all this fuss about, I can do as I please, this is only a dream. On this reflection, I stood up although my arm was still bleeding and I observed myself walking off into the distance pleased as punch.

Lucid dreaming can help you overcome anxiety dreams and nightmares because you know you are dreaming and therefore have nothing to fear. Dream images cannot hurt you.

Lucid dreamers can choose how they wish to respond to the events of the dream. For example, you can decide to face up to a frightening dream figure, knowing it cannot harm you, rather than try to avoid the danger, as you naturally would if you did not know it was a dream. This sense of control can transform the dream experience from one in which you are the helpless victim of frequently terrifying, frustrating, or maddening experiences to one in which you can dismiss, for a while, the cares and concerns of waking life.

Some people are able to achieve a level of mastery in their lucid dreaming where they can create any world, live any fantasy, and experience anything they can imagine. John has had lucid dreams regularly since the age of ten and they are a most important part of his life:

It can come as a shock to realize you are having a lucid dream, and this may lead to a sudden shift back to ordinary dreaming. However, it is possible to continue in the dream while remaining fully aware that you are dreaming and over time develop more and more dream control.

JOHN'S DREAM

With regard to everyday life I find I can rely on memories of lucid dreams, which are very vivid and quite unforgettable. These memories have helped me enormously and I tend to draw on them intuitively as they are needed. Highs and lows are somehow neutralized by them, and I feel stronger because of this. I see the ability to dream lucidly as a great opportunity to expand awareness, and it is available to anyone.

EXPANDING YOUR LUCID DREAMS

If you can recall being lucid in a dream, the next time you enter one try extending your range of control. The following visualization techniques are designed to help you develop your potential for lucid dreams.

• Try to fly or rise above the place of the dream setting.

• Move objects in your dream without touching them.

• Write a poem or explore a story idea that you will recall on waking.

• Adapt or completely change the direction in which your dream is going.

• Ask for a guide to help you in your journey.

• Travel to a country you have never been to before.

Complete control of lucid dreaming may take many years to accomplish. Some dreamers are more adept at lucidity in dreams than others, so just be patient and open to the possibility.

An alternative to lucid dreaming is to recall a dream while awake, and to "daydream" it further.

USING YOUR DREAMS AS PERSONAL ORACLES

Dreams exist in the threshold between the world of day and the world of night. In the darkened, separate world of dreams where we enter the underworld of caves and explore shadows, signs emerge to guide us. Our task is to learn to read the signs, to interpret the oracles of dreams. Here are some techniques that may help you.

WAKING DREAM VISUALIZATION

While you are awake, you can access part of your mind that comes to the fore in daydreaming or reveries. This will let you continue with a dream you want to develop or allow you to expand your awareness of characters or places you have known in the dream state.

Allow yourself 20 minutes to an hour for this visualization. At any time, if you feel uncomfortable or do not like the way in which it is developing, you can leave it and change the imagery. You are in control.

WAKING VISUALIZATION

1 Lie down in a comfortable place and close your eyes.

2 Consciously tense and relax the muscles in your body, starting with your feet and traveling to your head.

3 Let the images from the dream you wish to work on fill your mind. Go through the dream story.

4 Take three deep breaths, then focus on the character or place in your dream that you want to explore. Let yourself drift with the images that present themselves without seeking to control them or to censor them in any way.

5 Let the story continue and relax into the flow of events.

6 When you feel you have come to the natural end of the visualization, take your attention back to your body. Feel your weight resting on the surface on which you are lying. Open your eyes and remain where you are until your attention is fully back in your waking world.

7 Make a note of your visualization in your journal and use your Active Journal Work Techniques to interpret the waking dream.

Writing a positive affirmation in a notebook before you go to sleep may help you to heal negative thoughts.

SELF-HEALING THROUGH AFFIRMATIONS

An affirmation is a positive phrase that sends a message to your inner being. An affirmation is a powerful healing tool that reprograms negative messages from previous conditioning. If you have been told repeatedly that you are stupid or will never be successful, for example, those messages probably lodged in your psyche, became internalized, and convinced you that they were true!

The good news is that what has been learned can be unlearned, what has been programed can be reprogramed to give a positive, self-healing message that will empower you. Like prayer, your dreams can be used to help in this process of change. It is a way of focusing the mind for positive outcomes. Use your own internal voice to discover what affirmations you need and repeat them to yourself when awake. You can invent your own affirmations: use self-enhancing, positive phrases. Before you sleep affirm that you will have dreams to heal your mind, body, and spirit. Here are some affirmations you might like to try:

> • My dreams enhance every waking hour.
>
> • My dreams refresh and revitalize my life.
>
> • My dreams heal my aching heart.

PROBLEM-SOLVING IN DREAMS

If you ask for guidance, dreams can sometimes help you solve problems. In the Middle East, a special dream prayer, known as *istigara*, is said just before going to sleep to invite dream guidance. I use a similar practice with clients, using dream request cards; it is easy to do and has proved to be highly successful.

Dream request card

On a piece of cardboard or paper, do a simple drawing that represents your concern and write your dream request below it. Place this under your pillow before you go to sleep and record your dream on waking.

Anna, who drew a broken heart, wrote the question: "Why do my relationships always break down?" In the morning she recalled a dream in which she went to a party with some friends. Everyone, including Anna, was having a

• Before you sleep ask for guidance or support about a particular concern. Keep your request simple.

• Place a piece of paper or a notebook under your pillow with your request written down.

• On waking, write down any words or images that have come in your dream.

• Use the Active Journal Work Techniques to explore the answer you have been given.

• Consult a dictionary of myths and symbols to discover additional insights.

good time but then Anna found herself sitting outside alone. One of the group came to ask her to rejoin them but she refused. Once awake, she thought about the dream and realized just how often she backs off from close contact and isolates herself, making friendship hard to sustain. Her dream showed how much the breakdown of her relationships depended on her rejection of others rather than the other way around, as she had previously thought.

MICHAEL'S DREAM

If I have a problem I need to solve, I go to bed with the problem on my mind and repeat it over and over before falling asleep and then a few days later I'll dream about it. When I wake I write it all down, sort out the symbolism and then I seem to have a solution or warning.

1 *Write your problem on a piece of paper, cardboard, or in a notebook. A simple sketch may help you to focus on the problem.*

2 *Place your question under your pillow or beside your bed before you go to sleep.*

3 *When you wake, record your dream in your journal. Think about what the dream may be telling you.*

Exploring a dream landscape may symbolize a "vision quest" —a search for an answer to a question.

Dream clues

Your problem-solving dreams can take many forms. A voice may give you advice or an instruction that will resolve the difficulty. You may be shown a number of choices to solve your problem, or told to go ahead because everything will be fine. Dreams that have bright colors and vivid images may give clarity to the issue at hand.

Vision quest

The vision quest used by Native Americans has been adapted by others, for example present-day Reiki masters, who wish to discover answers to profound questions such as "What is my life path?", "How may I find wisdom?", "How can I know the divine?"

In the amazing Don Juan stories of Carlos Castaneda, the vision quest is called "hunting for power" or "meeting with the ally." The initiate wanders in the wilderness, fasting, meditating, and sleeping in order that he may dream of an answer to his query. This may involve meeting a special person, an ally or guide, and receiving insights that are life-transforming.

Setting up a dream group

When caring people gather to share dreams, they support each other and pool their knowledge of symbols, myths, language, and experience, thereby extending the skills available to the individual.

The groups I run are made up of about eight to ten people who meet every one or two weeks for three hours. Each person brings a dream or dream series to work on during the meeting. Of course, not everyone may wish to work on a dream at every meeting but there is still a great deal to be learned from listening to other people explore their dreamscapes. The first person to explore a dream first tells the dream narrative and if he or she has made a drawing it is shown to the group. The other members may ask questions to clarify the story or details. If any group member wants to give ideas to enrich the interpretation, he or she uses phrases such as "If this were my dream, I would…" This is a way of offering ideas without imposing interpretations. Group members use the Active Journal Work Techniques (see page 20) to explore the settings, characters, etc. of their dreams.

If you decide to set up a group, you will need to find a comfortable, private space, perhaps in each other's homes or in a community center, and arrange a suitable time to meet. The beginning and ending times need to be established so that members are sure of the boundaries; this adds to feelings of security. Ensure that you have negotiated the ground rules for how the group will work together and make a copy for each person. Some suggested ground rules are listed overleaf.

Waking visualizations can be used as part of your own adapted vision quest as you focus on your power to connect with the universe and link up with the transcendent that lies within each of us.

DREAM SHARING

Sharing your dreams with other people can be a truly rewarding experience. Whether it is in a one-to-one situation with a friend, lover, or family member, or in a structured dream group, there are enormous benefits.

Dream doubling

You may find that members of the dream group, or people close to you, share your dream themes. This may be because you share a common inherited experience or because you have a strong intuitive awareness of each other, even though it may never have been spoken about.

Human beings connect with each other in so many ways, that it is not surprising that we have the ability to share the same dreams.

Celine had an interesting dream-doubling experience as a young child:

GROUND RULES

- Each person's contribution is valued.

- Listen to each person's contribution; only one person should speak at a time.

- Suggestions about the meaning of another person's dream are offered, not inflicted.

- The dreamer is the person who truly understands the dream and will understand it when he or she is ready.

- This is a wonderful opportunity to share in a loving and supportive way, so sensitivity and caring are vital.

- Everyone agrees to maintain confidentiality, otherwise trust in the group will be jeopardized. Taking part in a dream group is an ideal opportunity to develop your interpretation skills and deepen your awareness of your self and your place in the universe.

CELINE'S DREAM

I was climbing a metal ladder into the sky. I was frightened because there was a roaring, angry sea beneath. The odd thing is that my mother and my mother's sister were talking about dreams one day, I was about 11 at the time, and my mother said, "There is one dream I get a lot and it always frightens me." She then proceeded to describe my dream. The really odd thing is that I knew before she started that it was going to be my dream and it was the same in every detail.

FURTHER INFORMATION

If you would like more information about dream groups or are interested in sharing your dream experiences and ideas about dreams and dreaming, please contact me. It is always a privilege and a pleasure to hear from readers.

Brenda Mallon
7 Didsbury Park
Manchester M20 5LH
England
email lapwing@gn.apc.org

Sharing dreams within a group can be a very rewarding and life-affirming experience.

☾ | Further reading

Boss, Medard, *The Analysis of Dreams*
(Rider, London, UK, 1957)

Cirlot, J. E., *A Dictionary of Symbols*
(Routledge & Kegan Paul, London, UK, 1962)

Cockell, Jenny, *Yesterday's Children,*
(Piatkus, UK, 1993)

De Becker, Raymond, *The Understanding
of Dreams* (George, Allen & Unwin Ltd.,
London, UK, 1968)

Dee, Nerys, *Your Dreams and What They Mean*
(The Aquarian Press, Thorsons, UK, 1984)

Faraday, Ann, *The Dream Game*
(Temple Smith, London, UK, 1975)

Fontana, David, *The Secret Language of Symbols*
(Pavilion, London, UK, 1993)

Fox, Matthew & Sheldrake, Rupert,
The Physics of Angels (Harper: SanFrancisco,
US, 1996)

Garfield, Patricia, *Creative Dreaming*
(Futura, London, UK, 1976)

Hall, Calvin, *The Meaning of Dreams,*
(McGraw-Hill, US, 1953)

Hall, Nor, *The Moon and the Virgin*
(The Women's Press, London, UK, 1980)

Hanger, Joan, *Wake Up to Your Dreams*
(Penguin. London, UK, 1997)

Jung, C. G., *Man and His Symbols*
(Aldus Books, London, UK, 1964)

Lethbridge, T. C., *The Power of the Pendulum*
(Penguin Putman, UK, 1989)

Mallon, Brenda, *Children Dreaming*
(Penguin, London, UK, 1989)

Mallon, Brenda, *Creative Visualization with
Color: Healing Your Life with the Power of Color*
(Element, Shaftesbury, UK, 1999)

Mallon, Brenda, *Dreaming, Counselling and
Healing* (Gill MacMillan, Dublin, Eire, 2000)

Mallon, Brenda, *Women Dreaming*
(HarperCollins, London, UK, 1987)

Parker, Julia & Derek, *The Complete Book
of Dreams* (Dorling Kindersley Living Series,
UK, 1995)

Siegel, Bernie, *Love, Medicine and Miracles*
(Arrow, UK, 1988)

Stevens, Anthony, *Private Myths: Dreams
and Dreaming* (Penguin, London, UK, 1995)

Wolpert, Lewis, *Malignant Sadness: The
Anatomy of Depression* (Faber & Faber, UK, 1999)

) | Useful addresses

**American Sleep Disorders
Association**
1610 14th Street, N.W.,
Suite 300, Rochester,
MN 55901, USA

**Association for the Study
of Dreams**
6728 Old McLean Village
Drive, McLean, Virginia
22101-3906, USA

British Sleep Society
PO Box 144, Wakefield,
Yorkshire
WF4 2XY, UK

PICTURE SOURCES

AKG London: 7t, 13bl, 56b, 89, 105t.
The Bridgeman Art Library: Archeologico Museo
Nazionale, Naples, Italy 100l; Bonhams, London, UK 65b;
British Museum, London, UK 12l, 71r; Bury Art Museum
& Gallery, Lancashire, UK 14; Museo Catedralicio,
Cuenca, Spain 79b; Christies Images 25; Fitzwilliam
Museum, University of Cambridge, UK 66l; Musee
Francisque Mandet, France 12r; Giraudon 57b; Index 55t;
Louvre, Paris, France 86; Oriental Museum, Durham
University, UK 26b, 84; Musee du Petit Palais, Avignon,
France 48-49b; Royal Ontario Museum, Toronto, Canada
111; Victoria & Albert Museum, London, UK 94.
Corbis: 27b, 58, 76; Paul Almasy 69; David Cummings:
Eye Ubiquitous 70t; Natalie Forbes 77t.
The Image Bank: Rob Atkins 70b; Gio Barto 69tl;
Mitchell Benn 31; Alfred Gescheidt 37; David H.
Hamilton 73t.

The Stock Market: David Aubrey 39b; Lester
Lefkowitz 44b; Jose Luis Peleaz Inc. 101b.
Tony Stone Images: Glen Allison 77b; Bruce Ayres
47, 71l; Jon Bradley 21c; Tim Brown 105b; Chris
Cheadle 46br; Andy Cox 53c; Ron Dahlquist 73b;
Ellen Dooley 73b; Chad Ehlers 68, 85; Scott
Goldsmith 33b; Rick Graves 21t; Jon Gray 45; Chris
Harvey 30b; Jason Hawkes 48tl; Wilfried Krecichwost
51b; Tony Latham 30c; G. Brad Lewis 73b; Joe
McBride 97; Will & Deni McIntyre 110; Myron 43b;
Jean Pragen 27t; Ed Pritchard 24r; R.K.G.
Photography 120; Rolf Schultheiss 6bl; Pete Seaward
6br; Mark Segal 73b; Jagtar Semplay 51b; Don
Smetzer 53t; David Stewart 62l; Stephen Studd 100br;
Bob Thomas 65t; Alan Thornton 46bl; Olney Vasan
90tl; Nick Vedros & Associates 6bc; Gary Vestal 43t;
Tony Wacker 41; Charlie Waite 108b; Paul Wakefield
73b; John Warden 33b; Kim Westerkov 63; David
Young-Wolff 102l.

The publishers would like to thank the following for help with photography:
Curiouser & Curiouser, Brighton, East Sussex, UK

My thanks to all the dreamers, clients, and workshop companions who told their dreams.
Without their openness and generosity in sharing their thoughts and dreams
I could not have written this book. My thanks and love to you all.

☽ | Index